Games, Crafts, & Creative Activities for **3- to 6-Year-olds**

Wonderplay, Too!

• cooking • science • music • games • art • dance •

from the **92nd Street Y** by Fretta Reitzes & Beth Teitelman

RUNNING PRESS
PHILADELPHIA • LONDON

© 2007 by 92nd Street Y
Illustrations © 2007 by Headcase Design
All rights reserved under the Pan-American
and International Copyright Conventions

Printed in the United States

*This book may not be reproduced in whole
or in part, in any form or by any means, electronic
or mechanical, including photocopying, recording,
or by any information storage and retrieval system
now known or hereafter invented, without written
permission from the publisher.*

9   8   7   6   5   4   3   2   1
Digit on the right indicates the number
of this printing

Library of Congress Control Number: 2007923811

ISBN-13: 978-0-7624-2863-2
ISBN-10: 0-7624-2863-5

Cover illustration by Headcase Design
Interior illustrations and design based on
   Wonderplay by Paul Kepple
Edited by Jennifer Kasius
Typography: Avenir and Clarendon

This book may be ordered by mail from the publisher.
Please include $2.50 for postage and handling.
But try your bookstore first!

Running Press Book Publishers
2300 Chestnut Street
Philadelphia, PA 19103-4371

Visit us on the web!
www.runningpress.com

A WORD OF CAUTION: As you do the activities described
in this book, please use good judgment and common
sense, and always keep safety in mind. The authors
and publishers of this book have no responsibility for
any unintended or improper application of any of the
suggestions in the book.

For our parents

who loved us when we were young children

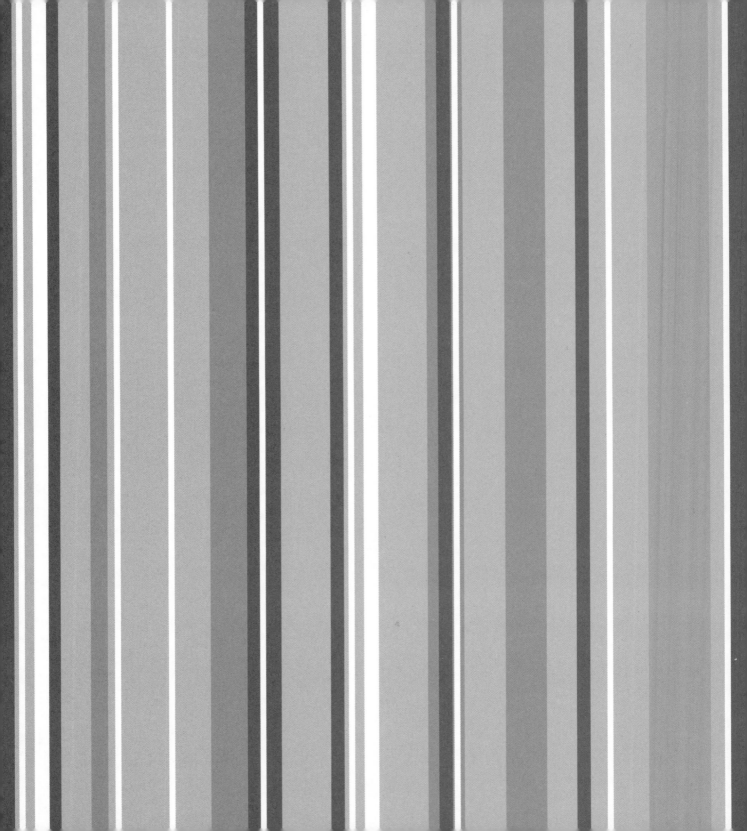

Contents

Introduction

~~~~~~~~~~~~~~~~

Welcome to the 92nd Street Y! Every day, hundreds of young children come through our doors. They arrive walking, on scooters, in strollers, on the back of their parent's bikes, by bus, subway, car, and taxi. The Y's bustling lobby is the gateway to our playrooms, art and dance studios, gyms, pool, and classrooms. All day long, our Y children have a wonderful time. They learn, grow, play, make friends, create, discover, and imagine. They make the Y their very own place. A parent once told us that her three-year-old would often say, "Let's go home to the Y!" And that is how our families feel about their time with us.

It is no surprise that so many families come to the 92nd Street Y to be part of our terrific programs for young children. After all, they have been coming through our doors since 1939 when the Y's nursery school first opened. During the 1960's with the emerging focus on early learning, the 92nd Street Y pioneered innovative, age-appropriate programs for young children in many content areas. Today, the Y's commitment to excellence and leadership in early learning continues. We have now been a nation-wide model for nearly seventy years visited by professionals from all over the world.

For more than a decade we have brought the 92nd Street Y Parenting Center to parents of infants and toddlers in *Wonderplay*. We continue to hear from many parents and professionals how useful and enjoyable this book is. Once again, we open our doors to your family. Join us with *Wonderplay, Too!* as we bring you all that the 92nd Street Y offers to children ages three to six. The activities in this book can be enjoyed at home, in your living room, kitchen, or back yard using everyday items you already have on hand and a few inexpensive, easy-to-find additions. *Wonderplay, Too!* is filled with ideas, recipes, projects, make-believe games, and practical tips to enjoy with your children throughout these early childhood years. We invite you to browse, pick, and choose what fits the moment and sparks your excitement and imagination.

Play Happy, Play Safe

~~~~~~~~~~

Your children are growing up and you have emerged from the years when you must be with them every minute. They now often play independently, and that is an important part of these early years. Nevertheless, parents continue to have a vital role in making sure their children are safe. As you use the activities in this book, be sure you have a safe and secure environment.

Because each section in this book spans a wide age range, consider the developmental readiness of your children and wait until they are able to handle a particular activity. Do not push them to participate in an activity that is beyond their physical ability or interest level. Use judgment about when to leave your children playing independently, always within earshot and checking in.

Begin by reading the manufacturer's age guidelines for all materials and equipment. Check the labels on paint, glue, and other art materials to ensure that they are nontoxic and safe. Use only child-safety scissors, and stay on hand to supervise. If adult scissors are needed, always keep them out of your children's reach and reserve them for adult use only.

When cooking with your children, do not use sharp instruments, utensils, or breakable containers. Use electrical appliances with adult supervision only. Adapt recipes to exclude items to which your children are allergic and read all labels thoroughly. Be sure to find out what food allergies any visiting friends may have. Remember, only adults use the oven and stove top.

When doing these activities outdoors, use judgment about adult supervision and what your role should be. Check all areas for potentially hazardous materials such as broken glass, poisonous plants, or animal traces. Be sure that everyone washes their hands when coming back inside.

You may often have other children, family or friends, at your home and may choose to do some of these activities with them. Remember to pay additional attention with children who are not your own, making sure that everyone stays safe and sound.

Common sense and caution go a long way to enjoying your time together with your children.

The Y's of It All

56

Why, where, when, how?" Is anyone more curious, inquisitive, and constantly questioning than a young child? Three-to six-year-olds are busy making sense of what they observe and experience in their expanding world of home, school, and community. They are trying to figure out who does what, how things work, why things happen, and how it all fits together.

**Where does the sun
go at night?**

When will I get bigger?

Why does it rain?

How do buildings stay up?

They are known for coming up with a variety of explanations, some right on target and others deliciously wild, inventive, funny, and uniquely theirs. They enjoy their growing understanding of how the world works and are eager to figure out how they fit in.

Your children, who love and need you above all others, also have important relationships beyond the family. In their daily lives, they interact and get to know many different adults such as your local librarian and pediatrician. They may have a favorite teacher or a special friendship with a next-door neighbor. Making friends with other children becomes especially meaningful as they learn to handle the ups and downs of friendships. Young children look forward to being with

> Try to read to your children every day. Have a few books with you to read wherever and whenever you can.

> Keep a dress-up box filled with shoes, hats, sunglasses, ties, beads, shawls, and whatever your children can use in their play.

their friends and playing together with great enthusiasm.

Young children also love becoming more independent, relish doing things on their own, and take great pride in their many new accomplishments. They are pleased with their increasing ability to understand and follow directions. They are more competent as they learn to put on their jackets, tie their shoes, comb their hair, pour their cereal and milk, ride their bikes, buckle their seat belts, recognize words, and read signs. They love when you notice what they can do and acknowledge how grown up they are becoming.

Three-to six-year-olds are on the move! They are running, jumping, climbing, hopping, dancing, and skipping with growing coordination and agility. Filled with exuberance, they are constantly busy, and it takes a lot of energy to keep up with them.

"The Y's of It All" is a collection of ideas, suggestions, and practical tips about day-to-day life with your three-to six-year-olds. As you read, pick and choose what feels right for your family. With a new idea or two, you can stay one step ahead of your energetic and curious children. Have fun and enjoy your time together!

Being Part of the Family

Throughout these years, your child is increasingly ready and able to participate in the daily routines that keep your family going. He sees you going about your everyday chores and may want to participate to show how grown up and competent he is. Young children often like being "part of the action" and included as important members of their family.

Include them in the daily routines of family life even though it will require some effort on your part. This is a good time to introduce them to many tasks and welcome whatever they can do to help. Have realistic expectations, anticipating that their interest may ebb and flow.

Some tasks are particularly suited for young children. Folding napkins, sorting and pairing socks, sweeping, and holding the dustpan can be great fun. Gradually, they can help you with pet care, watering plants, raking leaves, setting the table, unpacking groceries, washing the car, and sponging the kitchen counter. Like all family members, young children should continue putting their own personal belongings away. Be prepared to lend a hand as needed.

Family meals are wonderful opportunities for your children to be actively involved in family life. If dinnertime is not practical for everyone to eat together, consider alternatives such as breakfast, weekend lunches, or evening snack times. These are important times to talk and share. Every so often, your children can be the ones to plan these family meals. You might also cook something together for everyone to eat and enjoy.

Get Up and Go! Exploring Your Neighborhood and Community

By car and bus, subway and train, and on foot, these are great years for local adventures with your child as she is ready to discover more about the world. By now, you most likely have favorite destinations in your neighborhood that you visit together. These often include the nearest pet store, post office, firehouse, bank, library, farm, hardware store, and park. Perhaps your community also has a duck pond or zoo where you enjoy visiting the animals. There may be some special people at these places who give your child a warm hello and chat with you.

A young child's life centers on his family and home during the earliest years. Now, your child is ready to expand his knowledge of the neighborhood, local community, and world beyond. Visiting new places and meeting new people stimulates your child's curiosity and helps him understand his place in the world. This is an important step in your child's growing up.

Add to your list of destinations. Be aware of what might appeal to your child, be nearby, and contribute to her growing understanding of how the world works. Seek out interesting sculptures, statues and fountains, natural phenomena such as waterfalls and rock formations, gardens and parks, construction sites, and local landmarks. These are great years for first trips to historical sites that illustrate life in earlier times. Museums, even small ones without special exhibits for children, can be engaging as you and your child together choose something of interest to see.

Engage his imagination even before you leave home by sharing a few comments about where you are going and what you will do. Preparing for your visit and anticipating what you will see adds to the fun.

Short visits are best to keep your child's interest level high. Know your child and keep your excursions to a scale he can manage. Consider choosing one or two things to focus on, planning to return another time to see more. While on your visit, give your child a few quiet moments to take in what he is seeing. Parents sometimes offer more information than a child can absorb and a few thoughtful comments from you are sufficient.

Your child may or may not ask questions or want to talk about what he sees. Often a child's questions come several days later. Some children never ask questions or talk at all about what they have seen. Remember, your child takes it all in and learns from each experience in his unique way.

You can also enrich and extend your "trips" when they are over. Take a picture of what you saw, and keep a book of these excursions to look at from time to time adding pictures as you return to your favorites. As your child gets older, you may begin a scrapbook of simple "souvenirs" from your visits including pictures, ticket stubs, postcards, and brochures. These souvenirs can help you remember your trip and begin some great conversations about what you have seen and set the stage for a return visit.

～～～～～～～～～～～～～～～

Bring indoor activities outside to the backyard, park, or playground. Giving your child a larger open space adds a new dimen- sion to play.

Celebrate Holidays!

Holidays offer unique opportunities for joyful celebrations. They provide a way to preserve or create ongoing family rituals and traditions giving your child a treasure of memorable experiences. Children anticipate and look forward to these special days with enthusiasm. They now enjoy being part of the planning and preparations. You and your

child can have wonderful conversations as you share your own childhood memories of family holidays, talking together about past celebrations.

For young children, holidays are often challenging, with more stimulation and excitement than usual. Routines change, relatives and friends frequently visit, and parents may be distracted and less available. For parents, celebrations also involve extra energy, time, and work. With all of the preparation, these occasions can be overwhelming and exhausting for both you and your child. Bombarded by so many suggestions from television, magazines, and Web sites for making holidays "better than ever," there is often pressure to do more, when less is the way to go.

Consider some ways to minimize the stress and maximize the fun. Know yourself, your child, and your family, paying attention to what feels right for you. Spending excessive time and money beyond your means will not necessarily guarantee a perfect celebration but will add to your stress and exhaustion.

Including your child in the holiday preparations may help you all have a better experience. Make placemats and table decorations or cook one holiday dish together. Decorating place cards is a great way to keep your child engaged while you are busy with other preparations. Find a quiet moment to sit together and chat about who is coming and why they are important to your family as you write their names on the place cards. Your child will be happy and proud for everyone to see what he has contributed to the holiday.

Celebrate Birthdays!

As you know so well, children love to feel important and look forward to their birthdays with great pleasure. By now, they have experienced some birthday celebrations with friends and family. They are old enough to understand what a birthday means, to have some idea of what to expect, and to know that they will be the center of attention on their very special day.

Birthdays, with all of the anticipation and focus of attention, may be more than your child can handle. When planning a birthday party, keep it on a scale that is manageable so that your child is not overwhelmed. You may want to set aside a few of her birthday presents to open after the party or on another day. Often, simple tried-and-true solutions work best. Decorating party bags and cupcakes and group games such as freeze dancing and Simon Says can be the ingredients for a great birthday party.

Other ways to make birthdays special include having your child choose the family's menu for the whole day as you set some guidelines. Make a birthday crown to wear and a "Happy Birthday" sign. Remember to include quiet times during the course of the day. Reading favorite stories or simply talking together gives your child a chance to relax and settle before moving on to another exciting part of her special day.

Repeat, Recycle, Redo, Revisit!

There are many good reasons to repeat, recycle, redo, and revisit activities you have done before with your child. We all need "old favorites" in our repertoire as well as new challenges. Children need time to enjoy the familiar and predictable because it helps them to feel comfortable and competent. As you repeat activities over and over, there are many opportunities for exploration and discovery. Your growing children bring new thinking, skills, interest, and enthusiasm to what they have tried before.

Young children explore new activities in a very simple way. Over time, as they revisit the same activity, the activity has more depth. For example, your child begins painting as a two-year-old with one brush and a few colors. This basic form of painting may stay the same for awhile. As your child matures and is ready, painting involves new types of brushes and tools, more colors, different types of paint, and a variety of surfaces to paint on. Painting many times over and over again, your child develops fine motor skills and eye-hand coordination, as well as learning about color, texture, shape, and form, all while having fun doing what she has done many times before.

Let your child's interest and enthusiasm guide you. You may want to put an activity away for awhile. It will be there later for you to repeat, recycle, redo, and revisit when the time feels right.

Finding Time To Be Together

Your days as a parent are full and busy. Although young children can do more on their own, they still need your attention. Meals, laundry, cleaning, and errands as well as work, school, and other family responsibilities also require your time. It is often challenging for many parents to find time to play, explore new activities, and have fun with their children.

Even though it is difficult, finding time to be together is what counts most. Take a walk, look at something interesting outdoors, or just cuddle up and have a chat. When you cannot set everything else aside and must do household chores, involve your child in what you are doing. Helping you unpack the groceries, make a meal, or sort the laundry can be cozy times as you enjoy each other's company.

Whenever possible, turn off your cell phone, television, and e-mail, so that you are not distracted. Spending time together will lead to a more self-sufficient, independent, creative child and is well worth the effort.

Choosing Additional Classes

There is a wide variety in how young children spend their days. Many, but not all, are in some type of preschool, day care, or family home care program. Some parents also want their children to participate in additional classes that offer enrichment and new experiences. There are many choices, such as dance, swim, art, music, gymnastics, karate, and sports.

When choosing a class, look at your child's weekly schedule. Consider one additional class as a good way to begin. Although there are many wonderful activities to choose from, do not overdo it. Remember, young children need unstructured and unplanned time to play, explore, and relax.

Keep in mind the practical logistics including transportation to and from, who will accompany your child, class fees and extra expenses, and whether it works with your family's schedule. If an additional class is too difficult to fit into your week or will strain the family budget, revisit the decision at another time. These classes are not essential to your child's well-being.

If you decide to try a class, get recommendations from your child's teachers and other parents in your community. Look for programs designed for young children with their developmental needs in mind. You might want to talk with the director or teacher about what the class will be like for your child. Consider observing a few minutes of a class to see it in action. Look for program spaces that are safe and clean. Although some spaces will seem fancier and more state-of-the-art, remember that there can be a great class in a very modest setting. It is the teacher and the program that make the difference.

Each additional class for a young child introduces different adults, children, routines, and expectations. Even children who already attend preschool and day care programs need time to settle in and feel comfortable in a new setting. Pay attention to what your child says about the class and check in with the teacher to see how your child is doing. Enjoy your young dancers, artists, swimmers, gymnasts, musicians, or ballplayers as they share their excitement and enthusiasm with you!

Your Caring Child

Your young child is now ready to learn new ways to understand and respond to the needs of other people. Let her know that everyone sometimes needs special love and attention. There are many child-sized ways that children can express their feelings of concern and affection. Begin with your child's own community, including family members, classmates, friends, and neighbors. Help her make and send birthday and get-well cards for the important people in her life. Cook food together to bring to someone who is ill. Holidays are especially important times for your children to express their concern for others.

The world beyond your home also has an impact on young children. In the media and all around them, they hear about people beyond your local community who are in great need. Children want to do something to show that they care. Empower them by providing ways for them to help. Together you and your children can collect and donate food, outgrown clothes, or used toys and books as needed. These are concrete ways your child can participate and feel that he is making a difference.

Children this age have often saved up some money from birthday gifts, holiday gifts, and visits from grandparents and special family friends. As your children get older, encourage them to contribute some of this money to a community organization that your family uses. Consider your public library, community park, or local playground. Talk with your child to help her make a choice that best reflects what she cares about.

Be a Collector!

You have heard it said that one person's trash is another person's treasure. This is especially true when you want to engage a young child's creativity. Keep your eye open for everyday objects and interesting materials that can spark your child's imagination. All around you are items waiting to be recycled as active ingredients in your child's play, art activities, and scientific explorations.

Keep your collection growing. Your child will use these items more if they are accessible and inviting. Figure out the best way to organize and store these materials as space allows. Large plastic bins and shoe boxes work well.

Here is a basic list of things for you to have on hand to begin your collection:

- Egg cartons
- Milk cartons
- Plastic food containers, fruit trays, and bottles
- Paper towel and toilet paper rolls
- Tissue paper
- Wrapping paper and ribbons
- All shapes and sizes of cardboard boxes
- Oatmeal boxes
- Large buttons
- Fabric scraps and trimmings
- Yarn
- Magazines and catalogs

You can also collect these free items from local stores:

- Color strips from the paint store
- Carpet square samples
- Wallpaper sample books
- Cigar boxes

Screen Time: Television, DVDs, Computers, and Electronic Games

You are raising your children at a time when technology offers exciting possibilities for everyone. There are terrific Web sites to browse, movies to watch, games to play, digital photos to enjoy, and e-mails to answer. Use technology creatively with your children. It can help you stay in touch with family and friends, learn about the larger world, and have fun with interactive games and programs. The possibilities are limitless, and technology offers an exciting and enticing way to spend time together.

Parents need to be actively involved in choosing what their children see on the screen. Watch television and play computer games with them so that you know what they are seeing and whether it is appropriate. Be sure to avoid violent content and whatever may scare or confuse your child. Be aware that having the television on constantly may expose your child to unnecessary or disturbing information and visual images.

Young children often see things differently than adults. They do not always have a context for what they see or understand it accurately. The line between fantasy and reality is not yet firmly established for them. Make clear choices about what they watch and set limits based on what feels right for your child and family.

"Screen time" adds up! Parents also need to pay serious attention to the number of hours their children spend in front of a screen. Some "screen time" may be fine for your child and give you a chance to get other things accomplished. However, it is very easy to lose track of the accumulated hours your child is watching television or using the computer. Too many hours in front of a screen may mean that your child is missing out on important time for creative play and physical activity during these early years.

Although technology is exciting and enticing to young children, it also has clear limitations. Early childhood educators are especially concerned that too much "screen time" takes the place of active, hands-on learning. This results in less time for play and activities that nurture creativity, imagination, problem-solving, and social interaction. So enjoy some "screen time" together, always aiming for a thoughtful balance and variety of activities for your child.

More Than One: Sisters and Brothers

Many families grow to include more than one child, with a wide variety of ages among their children. Parents hope that their children will love and respect each other and get along. Relationships between brothers and sisters are complex, depending on age and gender difference, personality, and your family life. Although you may want your children to be close to each other, you cannot force them to feel this way. Along with affection and caring, there is likely to be competition, jealousy, and conflict, which constantly change over time. Understanding and acknowledging these ups and downs will be helpful to you all.

Encourage your children's relationship with each other by recognizing their individual per-sonalities and abilities. Keep in mind that your children of different ages will not always be ready for the same thing at the same time. Be realistic and adjust your expectations and plans accordingly. There will be times when your children can be together happily taking turns, sharing, and enjoying each other's company. Sometimes they will do this on their own, and other times you will need to help them. Let them know how much you enjoy seeing them getting along and having fun together. Your children will also need time apart to explore their individual interests and friendships with children outside of your family.

When your children are home together, choose activities that appeal to both toddlers and preschoolers and allow each child to work independently. They can have their own materials as they work side by side. Consider setting up play dough, paints, or collage materials. Cooperative activities such as cooking offer opportunities for everyone to participate. Dancing to music and listening to stories also work well.

Here are some suggestions to help you plan activities for your children of different ages. Children do best when they know what to expect. Set the stage by telling them what you all will be doing together. Assure them that everyone will have a turn and get to participate. Choose activities that your older and younger child will enjoy doing together. Be clear that each child's project or art work is his own and may not be touched by

anyone without permission. If your children did an activity together and had a great time, build on their success. Repeat it perhaps with some variation. There are sure to be activities you have tried with them that did not turn out well for one reason or another. Do not rule these activities out for the future. Try them again with your children at another time, and you may discover a new family favorite.

Young children are just learning about sharing space and materials. Keep this in mind especially when you plan an activity for your children to do together. Try using blue painter's tape to define an area on a floor or table where each child can have an individual work space. Placemats also work well for smaller projects. Sometimes it is helpful to children when the adult divides and distributes the materials.

Encouraging your children to get along and love each other takes time and thoughtfulness. Let them know that you understand that it is not always easy being the youngest who cannot keep up or the oldest who always has to wait. Tell them you love each of them and all of them and that everyone has a special place in your family.

Friendship: Playing Together and Sharing

Young children are learning what it means to have friends and be a good friend and enjoy each other's company. Most have experience playing together with children they meet in your neighborhood, the local playground, preschool, and day care. They have many social skills initiating and planning their own games as they play cooperatively. They use language more effectively to communicate. They genuinely look forward to seeing each other, bursting with energy and enthusiasm when they get together.

Whether at home or on the playground, there are many ways you can encourage and support your child as he learns about playing together and sharing with friends. Young children may need your help getting started and going over the "rules of the game." Although they will be playing more on their own, be aware of what is happening and be ready to step in. When they are having a hard time, give them a chance to talk it over. Switching to an activity that does not require sharing or following rules might help. Play dough, making a snack, or listening to stories are good ones to try. As their playtime comes to an end, let them know that it will soon be time to finish what they are doing and clean up together. Always try to end on a positive note.

Your child may find it hard to share her own toys and space. When a friend is coming over to play, give your child the option of putting away something new or very special that might be too hard to share. When you notice that your child and her friend are not getting along, it may be time to step in. Avoid taking sides. Should your own child be bossy, controlling, and unwilling to share, gently take her aside to talk privately and discuss it more after her friend leaves. Young children sometimes cannot play together successfully for too many hours. Know your child's limits, and plan accordingly.

In addition to many hours of playing together, there are other opportunities to help your child be a good friend. Consider delivering a homemade card, sharing something you cooked, or making a special birthday picture. It is endearing to watch your child learn what it means to enjoy having and being a good friend.

Young children have fantasy and make believe right at their fingertips. Enjoy their spontaneity and be playful along with them.

The Rainy Day Box

Days with young children sometimes seem endless. There are many hours to fill, especially if the weather is bad or your child is sick. It is fun to have a "Rainy Day Box" full of surprises for these occasions. Something fresh and different brings new energy and a welcome change to your day. Keep your "Rainy Day Box" tucked away and out of sight, reserved for only you to bring out when the day seems extra long.

Here are some ideas for a "Rainy Day Box." Include art supplies such as new paintbrushes, a fresh drawing pad, unusual markers, a package of stickers, or a container of play dough. Add new toys and books, music to listen to, or a movie to watch. Put in a small "unbirthday" present, as well as something your child has not used in a while. Saying "hello" to an old favorite can be fun on a day like this.

If there is a recipe that you would like to try with your child, put it away in the box. Add some new cookie cutters or an interesting kitchen utensil. Cooking is great for these occasions. Include musical instruments, a special dress-up item, or a small hand puppet.

You might also enjoy decorating your box together with your children. Remember to update your box every so often as they grow and their interests change. Be sure to include something special for each child in your family.

Your children will enjoy your "Rainy Day Box" when it appears out of nowhere at just the right moment. They love reaching in for a surprise and finding something unexpected. At the end of the day, return your "Rainy Day Box" to its secret hiding place for when you need it again.

Getting Started

～～～～～～～～

You know your children, what they like and enjoy, and which activities will appeal to them. Support their enthusiasm, curiosity, and interest in what they love to do. These are wonderful years to try all kinds of activities and move in new directions. Your budding artist might really enjoy playing soccer. Your agile athlete might also love to cook. Young children sometimes need encouragement to try new things. Help them discover other interests, talents, and abilities as more favorites are yet to come.

Have fun and enjoy many good times together!

Play: All Kinds and Lots of It!

A typical morning for a young child might include clumping around the house in oversized grown-up shoes, making up a silly song about spring rain, building a towering castle out of fluffy pillows, scribbling chalk lines with many colors on the sidewalk, and running happily back and forth around two trees. Although seemingly without any purpose, it is a young child busy at work inventing, creating, imagining, and exploring. It is time well spent playing.

Play, and lots of it, is the most important activity for young children. Through play, they learn about the world and try to figure out how it works. Taking in all that they observe and experience, young children process an enormous amount of information. They are continually building their knowledge and understanding. Putting it all together and thinking it over, they reach their own variety of conclusions. Play is also a creative outlet for a young child's active fantasy and imagination. Play contributes to their sense of mastery and competence and gives a young child joy, pride, and a growing sense of self.

Play and language are closely connected. While busy at play, young children use language to express their feelings, create and tell stories, explain the rules of a game, and communicate with friends. Rhymes, word games, puppet shows, and storytelling all contribute to your child's language development. Language is also used while they are thinking about what they are doing. The connection between play and language is especially important as young children get ready to read and write.

> There is no "right" or "wrong" way to play. Welcome your child's creativity, playfulness, and imaginative view of the world.

Children thrive when they have a lot of time for play that is not structured or programmed. Young children benefit from unhurried time that allows them to play without being rushed. They need to create, explore, and invent at their own pace. Be sure to provide ample time at home for play.

Nurture your child's play by setting the stage. Blocks, dress-up clothes, stuffed animals, puppets, cars and trucks, dolls and miniature figures, and picture books all stimulate a child's imagination as he invents his own world and creates his own stories. Appreciate these wonderful playtimes and join in the fun. Your child might invite you to be a customer in his store, the audience for a puppet show, a guest at the tea party, and a patient in the doctor's office. Remember, it is your child's playtime, not yours, and there is no right way to play store, puppet show, tea party, or doctor.

So follow your children's lead as they head for play, all kinds and lots of it!

PLAYING WITH WORDS

Young children love to talk! They generally have a lot to say and are eager to tell you what is on their minds talking freely and playfully. They give long explanations about why you should read another bedtime story or a complete description of what their imaginary friend did that day. They will tell you every detail about their skinned knee or what happened in the playground. They often combine reality and fantasy into stories full of delightful twists and turns, trying out new ideas and words. Listen and play along as your child enjoys "playing with words."

LET'S MAKE-BELIEVE!

Pretend play is the heart and soul of being a young child. Everything they feel, see, do, hear, read, and watch in their everyday experience is woven into their make-believe play. Fueled by their imaginations, fantasies, and creativity, young children play with enthusiasm and gusto as this pretend play belongs to them. When playing "make-believe" young children continually blend one theme into another. Playing "house" turns into playing "firefighter" when the house catches fire and then turns into playing "restaurant" when the fire is out and the hungry firefighters need to eat. Children

Sometimes your child may want to do the same thing and play the same game over, and over, and over again! Although you may get bored, your child is most likely mastering new skills and having fun.

usually begin make-believe play on their own. Sometimes an idea from you helps get them started or enhances their play along the way.

Young children's "make-believes" frequently include playing house, firefighter, police, restaurant, tea party, office, wedding, doctor, new baby, school, forts and hiding places, zoo, store, and taking a trip. Kings and queens, fairy princesses, superheroes, castles and dragons are also part of fantasy play. Your children will have their own favorites.

Here are some examples of how you can encourage their play. Keep a dress-up box handy. Have toy dishes and paper plates for playing house, restaurant, and tea party. Play dough makes wonderful pretend food. Empty food boxes can be used to play supermarket. Cartons of different sizes make stoves, forts and hiding places, fire trucks, police cars, and airplanes. Play office or school with pads, pencils, rubber stamps, and paper clips. Paper flowers, a piece of tulle, and a man's jacket start a wedding. Play money can be used for playing

store and restaurant. Wrapping paper rolls turn into fire hoses, magic wands, and swords with special powers. Chalkboards can be used for school and restaurant.

WATER, WATER, EVERYWHERE!

Water play excites and delights young children. Pour and measure, sink and float, spray and splash, and enjoy playing with water. Fill a sink, bucket, or plastic bin with water to play inside or outside. Keep a small collection of plastic pitchers and spray bottles, measuring cups, funnels, strainers, corks, sponges, and bubbles. Your children can choose a few items to play with each time. Dolls, toy boats, and plastic animals offer possibilities for imaginative play with water.

Your child uses fantasy and make-believe to make sense of what she is learning about the real world. Playing store, school, and house gives her a chance to organize and understand new information.

COUNT AND DO

Take out a set of dice and get ready to roll. The first player rolls the dice and counts the number that comes up.

30

Let your children "read" to you by turning the pages and telling the stories they know so well from hearing them over and over again.

The second player has to think of an action and repeat the action the number of times on the dice. For example, actions can include clapping hands, wiggling your nose, jumping, singing a song, repeating a word, or reciting a nursery rhyme. Take turns and enjoy the fun as your children count and follow directions.

THE NAME GAME

There are different ways to play a matching game using the names of people in your family. You will be making five cards for each person's name. Write the name clearly one time on each card. Use big letters. Three-by-five index cards work well. Here is one way to play: Put out one card with each name face up. Shuffle the remaining cards. Your child now turns them over one by one placing each new card on the matching name card. Here is another way to play: Shuffle all of the cards, turn over the first card, and put it out face up. Turn over the next card. If it is a match, place it on the matching name card. If it is not, start a new pile with the new name card. Keep going until the nd of the deck. For younger children, you can begin this game by writing one letter on each card. For older children, add the names of other family members and friends to your deck.

Shoeboxes are just the right size to make garages for miniature cars and trucks, little houses for toy figures, and zoos for small animals. Cut doors and windows. Build a whole town by connecting your shoebox buildings, using tape for roads.

TEDDY BEAR PICNIC

Today is the day the teddy bears have their picnic! Gather your stuffed animals and invite your friends to bring a favorite along. Spread out your picnic blanket in the backyard, the park, or right in the middle of your living room floor. Real or make-believe, pack your lunches and a treat for each bear. Bears often enjoy play dough treats made especially for them by young children. Sing songs together, tell all of the bears a story, play games, and have a great time at your picnic.

To play restaurant or store, use the play money from a board game. You can also make your own with paper and markers or on the computer.

NAME THE OBJECT

To play "Name the Object," place twelve small objects that the players are familiar with several inches apart. For younger children, you might start off with fewer objects and name each one. Every player takes a close look. Next, cover all of the objects with a cloth or towel. There are different ways to play. Take turns naming one object that is under the cloth until the players have named them all. Play again adding more objects as you go. Here is a variation for older children: One player describes something about one of the objects, such as what color it is or what it is used for. The second player has to name the object described.

WHAT IS MISSING?

You will need at least two players for this memory game. To play "What is Missing?" collect eight to ten small objects that your child recognizes and can name. Spread them out several inches apart. All of the players should take a good look. The first player covers her eyes while the second player takes away one object and puts it out of sight. The first player must now guess, "What is Missing?" Take turns. Older children who are more experienced with memory games might enjoy some variations. Try taking more than one object away. After a few rounds, substitute a new object or two for the ones you have been using. Add more objects as the game continues.

SPECIAL SPACES & HIDING PLACES

Young children delight in cozy, child-sized places that are theirs alone. They love the privacy and sense of ownership, inviting only their friends, and maybe even you, inside. Together you can build a place for your child to engage in hours of imaginative play as these special spaces evolve into tents, playhouses, spaceships, trains, and castles.

Unleash your creativity to make a special play space with sheets, towels, corrugated cardboard, oversized cartons from air conditioners or refrigerators, and heavy-duty tape. Sheets draped over tables or taped between two walls are a great way to begin. Cut windows and doors in an appliance carton and decorate the inside and outside to add to the fun. Old bathroom rugs can be added as magic carpets. Your child will do the rest, choosing an assortment of what to have inside, changing it as his imagination takes him on new adventures.

You won't find a "special space" all boxed and ready to buy in your local toy store. It exists only when you create it together and your child brings it to life with her vivid and unique imagination.

You can buy extra sets of dice in toy and stationery stores and use them for various counting games.

Young children love to make puppets talk and come alive. A large cardboard box makes a great puppet theater. Make a video of the puppet shows so that you can enjoy watching them together.

PICTURE MEMORY

Young children love to create their own games, and this one is fun to make and play. Cut out ten different pictures of specific objects from magazines and catalogs. Glue each picture on a four-by-six-inch index card. These pictures might include foods, cars, appliances, animals, or toys. To play, lay the cards out with the pictures facing up. Take a good look to remember where each object is located. Turn the cards over in their places. The first player names an object. The second player has to find the card with that object and turn it over. Take turns. Play again, rearranging the cards. Older children can make a version of this memory game with pictures in one category. These categories might be animals, foods, clothing, or whatever they choose.

ONCE UPON A TIME

"Once upon a time" begins the story you are about to tell together. Everyone takes turns. The first storyteller starts with "Once upon a time," and begins to tell a story, stopping after a minute or so. The next storyteller adds more to the story. The story grows and unfolds as everyone takes a turn. Continue until "The End." Younger children may tell simple short stories, and older children may embellish and add more details. These made-up stories can be about anything and everything, real or imaginary. The same story might go on for a few days, weeks, or even longer, with new characters and adventures added.

CREATE YOUR OWN BOARD GAMES

Use this easy-to-make board to create your own board games. Begin with a sturdy piece of poster or foam board at least eighteen by twenty-four inches. Create a game path by drawing a long, winding line that twists and turns around the board. Make sure the game path has a clear start and finish. Next, make stopping places along your game path with colored stickers. Put the stickers along the game path, leaving some space between each one. Mark the "Start" and "Finish" places with an extra large sticker or a cluster of stickers. Add interest to your board with a few special stickers along the game path. You can also add some special directions to your board, such as "Move Ahead One Space." Your children will enjoy decorating the board. Collect a game piece for each player using small toys, erasers, buttons, shells, or stones. You will also need a set of dice or a spinner.

Now let the playing begin! You can invent many games for this all-purpose board. Younger children can play a number game by rolling dice and moving their game piece the right number of spaces. You can also make a set of small playing cards using the same stickers you used to make the board. Put one sticker on each card. Each player picks up a card and moves their game piece to the next sticker on the path, matching the sticker on their card. For older children, game cards can include words to read, numbers to add, and simple directions to follow. Be inventive and create many new games for your board.

CAN YOU FIND IT?

Here is a game to play with your children to get them thinking: Choose an object familiar

Board games are a great way for young children to learn about sequencing, taking turns, following rules, and playing to the end of the game. Before they know how to play by the rules, young children enjoy playing with the pieces and making up their own versions of the game.

~~~~~~~~~~~

Visit your local library often and get to know your librarian. Borrowing and returning library books can become a special part of your routine together. There will also be books, media, story hours, and special programs to enjoy at the library.

to your child. Describe one thing about it. It might be its color, what it does, or how it is used. Next, your child finds something that fits the description. For example, "I am thinking of something you draw with." Your child can find a pencil, marker, or crayon. As the game continues, describe two things about an object, giving your child more to think about. "I am thinking of something you draw with that is yellow." Now your child must find a yellow pencil, marker, or crayon. For younger children, keep the descriptions clear and simple. For older children, increase the challenge by adding more details to your descriptions. Once your children understand the game, try switching roles and give them a chance to get you thinking!

DEAR EVERYBODY!

Write a letter to get a letter! There are many opportunities for your children to "write" and send letters. Your children dictate their "letters" for you to write down. Write to family near and far, your friendly next-door neighbor, the librarian who helps you choose books, or a special friend. Everybody is delighted to receive "mail" from young children and usually answers. Your children can "write" letters, birthday cards, and thank-you notes. Along with letter writing, they can design their own stationery either on the computer or with markers, stickers, and crayons. Whether with paper and pencil or by e-mail, letter writing is a terrific way to communicate with words. So write a letter, address the envelope, put on a stamp, and drop it in the mailbox. Before long, your children will hear you say, "There's something in the mail for you!"

READ AND DO!
DO AND READ!

Connect the books you read to real life experience and real life experience to books. When you read a book about shapes, go on a shape hunt around your house, or cut out shapes to make a picture. After reading Halloween stories, cut up a pumpkin to see what is inside, bake pumpkin bread, or go to a pumpkin farm. When you visit the zoo, read books about animals and animal stories. Before and after your child's check-up, read books about going to the doctor. Books offer wonderful opportunities for young children to learn more about the world around them and enjoy their real life experiences.

BOOK DOCTOR

Books get lots of wear and tear. Become "Book Doctors," fixing and repairing your books. Give your books a "check-up" by examining the pages and spines. Use transparent tape for the ripped pages and reinforce the spines and covers. When your books are "healthy" again, your children can organize them. Younger children may sort their books by size or shape. Older children might want to categorize their books by subject. Being a "Book Doctor" gives young children experience caring for and respecting books. Every so often, as your books get more wear and tear, give them another "check-up."

BOOKMARKERS

You will never lose your place in the middle of a great story when you make your own bookmarker. Cut poster board or cardboard into strips at least two inches wide or use large unlined index cards. Decorate both sides with stickers, markers, and crayons. Older children can add their names. Covering bookmarkers with clear contact paper helps them last longer. A personalized bookmarker makes a great present.

TODAY STORIES

It is fun at the end of a busy day to remember what you did. With paper and pencil, or at the computer, sit down together and start your story of the day with "Today I . . . " Finish the sentence with something you did. As your children recall all that happened, write down what they say. Younger children may dictate a short "Today Story." Older children often recall a sequence of the day's events with lots of detail. Be sure to write the date on every "Today Story" and create a folder or notebook for them. Enjoy reading these stories together, and as they get older, your children can read them to you.

PACK YOUR SUITCASE

Young children love to pack their suitcases and enjoy playing "Pack Your Suitcase" games. Here is a version for younger children. Get out a bag to pack. Take turns. The first player

Even before your children are ready to play card games, a deck of playing cards is handy for matching, counting, and sorting. Sort them by color, suits, and numbers.

gives a clue describing something to pack. The next player has to find that item and pack it in the bag. For example, the first player says, "I am packing something to keep my teeth clean," and the next player might find a toothbrush or toothpaste to pack. Older children can play a memory game version of "Pack Your Suitcase." The first player says, "I packed my suitcase and put in my pajamas." The next player says, "I packed my suitcase, put in my pajamas, and my sunglasses." The game continues with players taking turns, adding new items and remembering the sequence until the imaginary suitcase is full.

THE "I MADE IT, I DID IT" MUSEUM

Proud of what they have made and done, your children now have a variety of wonderful science experiments, sculptures, drawings, stories, and instruments to share with other people. Create a "museum" together to exhibit a few of their favorites. Choose a place in your home for their museum so that it can stay open for a few days. A museum might be as simple as a few items displayed on a table. Your children may want to add labels identifying each object, make "Do Not Touch" signs, make

admission tickets, have a snack bar, and give tours! Invite a friend or two to visit. Be sure to be first in line at your child's "I Made It, I Did It" museum whenever the exhibit changes.

YOUR VERY OWN BOOKS

Young children love to make their very own books. Plain paper can be used for the inside pages. Construction paper works well for front and back covers. For smaller books, fold a piece in half. For larger books, use two pieces of construction paper for the covers. When your children have assembled the inside pages and covers, staple them together. You can also punch holes along the side of your book and sew the cover and pages together with yarn or ribbon. Young children also like to make their own small notepads in the same way, attaching the papers across the top.

Now that your children have made their very own books, it is time for them to fill the pages. These first books are very special. Your children will decorate the covers, dictate their own stories, draw pictures, add photographs, and make scrapbooks. As they learn to read and write, they may use their books to practice letters, numbers, and words. Before long, your children will have a library of their very own books.

Art Smarts in Action!

There is no telling what will happen when a young child becomes a working artist and sits down with paint, glue, brushes, and paper of all sizes and shapes. Given plenty of time and an interesting variety of materials, young children exercise their artistic muscles in a uniquely expressive way. They become engrossed in the process, using imagination, intelligence, and creativity. Over time, young children grow as artists and their art making becomes more complex and richer in detail. The final product may be exactly what they planned or turn out to be entirely different. Whatever the outcome, it is the process of art making that matters most.

Art making for young children includes painting, print-making, drawing, sculpture, and collage. There are many different ways to do each one, and combining them expands the creative possibilities. Often young children play around with various art materials just to see how they work and what they can do. All this experimentation has a large role in art making and needs to be encouraged. It is also important not to rush this process, and allow plenty of time for your young artist to concentrate and develop a sense of accomplishment and self confidence.

Keep some basic art supplies on hand. Collect interesting found objects for art making. Because art materials can be messy, set guidelines for where your children can use them as well as for cleaning up. Sometimes your children may want to work on their own. Other times they may choose to work nearby as you keep each other company. Art making works well when children of different ages are together and everyone can be an artist. Remember that your help may be needed at various times.

Talk with your children about their art making. Comment on the color, shape, texture, size, patterns, and lines that you observe in their art. Ask them to tell you about what they are working on rather than asking them, "What is it?" These art conversations give them a chance to put what they are thinking and doing into words.

Stir the paints, pour the glue, sharpen the drawing pencils, and enjoy what happens when your children put their art smarts into action.

Here are basic materials to have available:

- Tempera paint
- Watercolors
- Brushes of various sizes
- Clay or plasticine
- Yarn
- Glue and glue sticks
- Construction paper

- Assorted types and sizes of papers
- Crayons
- Pencils and erasers
- Markers
- Fabric crayons
- Paper plates

- Clear contact paper
- Scissors for children
- Tape (masking, plastic, and various colors)
- Stapler
- Pipe cleaners

~~~~~~~~~~~~~~~~~~~~

Found objects:

- Corks
- Buttons
- Paper towels rolls
- Paper scraps
- Styrofoam containers

- Berry baskets
- Greeting cards
- Ribbon
- Packing materials
- Fabric scraps

- Egg cartons
- Assorted boxes
- Magazines

~~~~~~~~~~~~~~~~~~~~

Art Conversations:

"I like the lines you made here."

"You made a big shape in that corner."

"I love the colors you chose."

"Do you want to add anything?"

"I see you made an interesting pattern."

"You have built it so tall."

"Is there anything in the collage box you want to use?"

~~~~~~~~~~~~~~~~~~~~

41

PLAY DOUGH

If making and using play dough is already part of your repertoire, keep on going! Children enjoy play dough for many years. If you have not yet begun, this is a great time to start.

Play dough is readily available either in stores or homemade. Both versions are easy to use, inexpensive, versatile, and engaging. Young children especially enjoy feeling the texture of play dough. They love to squeeze, push, pound, roll, and flatten it. And you might enjoy playing along as well.

You can make play dough easily at home. As your children get older, making play dough becomes a really intriguing activity with an element of science. You can talk about what happens when you mix wet and dry ingredients, how heat changes the mixture, and what you observe when color is added.

Homemade play dough keeps for many weeks when it is stored in a sealed plastic container. Although making it with your child is great fun, it is also a good idea to have some on hand ready to use when you need it.

You can use play dough on any washable surface. A countertop or tabletop works well, as does a plastic tablecloth spread out on the floor.

For young children, a chunk of dough the size of a tennis ball is good to start. Fingers are the best molding tools. You can also add miniature rolling pins, plastic cookie cutters, or a small, lightweight toy hammer. A garlic press is fun to use, too. You and your children are sure to think of other tools that are interesting to try.

To clean up play dough, get rid of any dry, crusty pieces from your supply before you put the play dough away. Use a scraper or textured nylon cleaning pad to scrape off your work surface. If you reserve a plastic tablecloth for play dough, it is not necessary to do a total cleanup. Simply throw away the dry bits and fold up the cloth for next time. Be sure to clean tools completely so that dry pieces of play dough do not get mixed in the next time you use them. Check the bottom of your shoes before you walk through the house!

> Some young children do not like getting their hands dirty, while others really enjoy it. Be sensitive to your child when considering paints, glue, play dough, and other messy materials.

Cooked Play Dough

1 cup flour

½ cup salt

2 teaspoons cream of tartar

1 tablespoon oil

1 cup water

Food coloring

1. Mix dry ingredients together in a sauce pan.
2. Add wet ingredients and mix together.
3. Cook over a low to medium flame.
4. Stir constantly to prevent scorching, until the mixture forms into a ball, no more than five minutes.
5. Knead until smooth.
6. Store in a sealed plastic container or refrigerate.

You can also make this recipe without the food coloring. You can then add food coloring as you knead, and observe the process of the white dough changing color together.

Uncooked Play Dough

Uncooked play dough can be made quickly with ingredients you have on hand and children can be part of the process. This is a great recipe to make when friends come over to play. Uncooked play dough does not keep as long the cooked version, and what your children make with it will crumble more easily.

2 cups flour

1 cup salt

1 cup water

Food coloring

1. Mix together flour and salt.
2. Add a few drops of food coloring to the water.
3. Add water and stir into dry ingredients.
4. Knead it together thoroughly. It may take a few minutes for the dough to form.

PLAY DOUGH SCULPTURES

Now that your children know how to make and use play dough, there is a lot to do with it. They can make free-form sculptures and add different materials such as beads, buttons, feathers, stones, or twigs. Once dried, these sculptures can be painted. Your children may want to create a group of these sculptures. You can glue the sculptures onto a piece of wood or small box to create a base for them. Older children may begin to sculpt their play dough into animals, cars, boats, people, or other objects from their everyday experience. Cooked play dough works best for these sculptures.

CRAYONS, DRAWING PENCILS, AND MARKERS

Young children love to draw and often spend lots of time with pencil and paper. Dots, lines, scribbles, and squiggles turn into faces, houses, dogs, trees, cars, and rainbows as their drawings gradually become more representational. Always, always, always have plenty of crayons, drawing pencils, markers, and paper available. Drawing is an activity that children can initiate on their own. You do not need to set it up to get them started. Keep drawing supplies within their reach. Remember that young children can be happy drawing on the back of an envelope, in a small spiral notebook, or on a piece of scrap cardboard. Take some drawing supplies along wherever you go!

Keep an assortment of small, inexpensive house-painting brushes on hand to use for various activities. Look for other interesting painting tools such as sponges on sticks and small rollers.

SCRATCH PICTURES

Crayons come in many shapes, sizes, and colors. Take a piece of drawing paper. The first step is to cover the entire paper, edge to edge, coloring it with crayons. It can be a design of any kind, using one color or many. Next, color over the entire paper with black crayon covering the first layer of crayon. Then, create a design or picture by taking a pencil, popsicle stick, or key to scratch through the black layer of crayon until the bottom layer

It is your child's artwork, not yours! Let your child be the artist. There is no right or wrong way to be creative with art materials.

of color shows through. Wonderful color will emerge from your scratch picture! It is fun to cut your scratch picture into an interesting shape and use leftover pieces for a collage or to add to a mobile.

Painting Basics

Young children love to paint! Painting, with watercolors or tempera, with thin and thick brushes, on all sizes and shapes of paper, standing at an easel or sitting at a table, is an activity with wonderful variety. Keep a few basic painting materials on hand including different sizes and kinds of brushes, an old shirt or smock, the primary

Never use glitter with young children. It is unsafe. Glitter consists of tiny metal pieces and can be harmful to your child's eyes.

Store materials that are unsafe for children to use alone in a safe place. These include scissors, staplers, pipe cleaners, and tape dispensers. Be sure to use only nontoxic glue, paint, crayons, and markers.

colors of tempera and a small watercolor set, a plastic container for water, and a large cleanup sponge. Keep a supply of nine-by-twelve and larger sized paper. A plastic tablecloth or shower curtain liner can be used to protect your floor or table.

With tempera paints, start by setting out a small amount of each color. Each color needs its own brush. Mixing colors is an important part of painting. Paints can be mixed directly on the paper or combined in small paper cups. Make sure to keep a container of clean water nearby for cleaning brushes and wiping up drips.

Watercolors come in boxed sets or in small separate cakes of each color. These cakes are often easier for young children to use. Usually, one brush is used for watercolor painting so the water needs to be changed frequently. You might want to show your child the technique that works well with watercolors. Dip the brush in water, tap it on a sponge to absorb the excess water, dab the brush in the paint, and then bring it to the paper to paint. White paper works best for watercolors with young children.

Children often say,
"I don't know how to draw it,"
and sometimes they really don't.
You may need to show them
on your paper or a separate
piece of paper.

Your child can paint on many different surfaces using different tools. Paint on large and small paper, boxes, textured cardboard, newspaper, wrapping paper, brown craft paper, and white shelf paper. Cut the paper into different shapes. Try painting with house painting brushes or small rollers.

Be inventive and creative, and try painting in many different ways.

FINGER PAINTING

Finger painting is messy and worth it! Roll up your sleeves and put on your smocks. Use nontoxic finger paints you buy or make it by mixing tempera paint with a bit of liquid dishwashing soap. Shiny shelf paper can be used for finger paints, or you can buy finger paint paper at an art supply store. Wet the paper with a sponge, add a small amount of paint, and get those fingers moving. You can also finger paint on a cookie sheet or in a large shallow baking pan just for fun. Use a disposable aluminum pan or one that you reserve for art work. Fingertips, knuckles, and nails all vary the lines and designs. Keep paper towels and a bucket of water handy for clean up. Consider finger painting outdoors.

Add variety to your child's artwork by using paper other than the standard rectangle. Cut circles and other interesting shapes from different kinds of paper.

STRING PAINTING

All types of string, yarn, ribbon, and twine add pizzazz and make painting a different experience. Use strings that are six to eight inches long. Here are two ways to string paint. Dip a string in tempera paint and move, glide, twist, turn, and tap it on paper. To make your string painting more interesting, use another color and another kind of string. You can also string paint by painting with tempera and then moving string through the paint to create a design.

SPONGE PAINTING

Sponges come in different textures and sizes. Look for an assortment to use as painting tools. Cut the pieces into a comfortable size for a young child's hand. Use one sponge for each color, and have a few pieces available for color mixing. Dip the sponge into tempera paint and stamp it on the paper. Try using the sponge in different ways, dabbing it, gliding it, swirling it, all creating patterns of color and texture. Sponges can be cut into shapes and used to print with paint.

COLLAGE, COLLAGE, COLLAGE

Collage is created by assembling and arranging different materials. Keep your collage box full as you add whatever buttons, yarns, feathers, trimmings, fabric, and other items come your way. With some glue and a sturdy piece of paper or cardboard for a background, you are set to begin. You might want to help your children choose which

materials to use from your collage box. Older children might spend more time planning and arranging their design and adding other kinds of paper.

TORN PAPER COLLAGE

Paper is all around you and can be used as an art material. Collect various kinds of papers as they come your way. Include wrapping paper, newspaper, magazines, catalogs, tissue, packing paper, and shopping bags, always looking for interesting textures, colors, and designs. Set out a sheet of paper to use as the background. Then choose some papers from your collection for your child to tear into different shapes and sizes. Notice the newly torn edges. Create a collage by arranging, overlapping, and layering the pieces. Move the pieces around until you create a design you want to keep. Hold your collage pieces in place with glue or by painting over it with a glue wash. To make a glue wash, mix a

To help your children "loosen up" and be ready for art making, give them a "scribble page." It can be a large piece of paper, newspaper, or a paper bag to practice on first.

solution of water and liquid glue. Use a clean paint brush to paint over the pieces, covering them all completely. You can also use a glue wash to add more pieces and painting each one as you add it. Be careful not to use too wet a brush when you paint.

PRINTMAKING

Young children can be great printmakers! Printing can be done with corks, potato mashers, slotted spoons, cookies cutters, small toys, sponges, plastic bottles and lids, blocks, and spools. Look around to find other objects to use. You can print starting with one object and one color at a time. Vary the size and type of paper you print on. Let one color dry and print with another. Use more than one object to enrich your print. A simple way to print is to pour some tempera paint into an aluminum pan. Keep a folded paper towel next to the pan to absorb excess paint from the object before using it to print. Printed paper makes beautiful wrapping paper for your child to share.

CREATIVE COMBOS: PAINT, PRINT, COLLAGE, AND DRAW!

As young children have repeated experience with painting, printmaking, collage, and drawing, they are ready to combine these techniques. Older children can wait for paint and glue to dry, look at their "work in progress," and plan the next step. They might take several days to finish. Perhaps your child will paint an egg carton. When the paint dries, he might draw on it with markers and glue small pieces of fabric scraps to the

> Keep a roll of brown wrapping or craft paper on hand. Stationery and office supply stores have all types of paper on rolls to be used for larger-sized projects.

> An assortment of large plastic bins and containers can be used to organize and store art materials. Keep several on hand to use as needed.

It is not necessary to buy a closetful of art materials and kits. Use your imagination and look at basic materials in new ways.

bottom of each compartment. Next, he might print some shapes on the top of the box and glue on interesting pebbles or buttons. His egg carton has been transformed! Encourage these creative combinations as your children explore mixed media.

STARRY NIGHT

Look at the night sky full of shining stars and the moon. Next, come indoors and make your own indoor starry night. A grown-up cuts out some stars, about six to eight inches across, from heavy paper, poster board, or cardboard. Then cut out whatever shape moon you observed. Now your child begins by painting the stars and the moon. When the paint is dry, glue on collage materials. Add some small pieces of aluminum foil so your stars will twinkle. Attach your stars and moon to the ceiling using two-sided tape or Fun Tack™. You can make more stars another time to add to your indoor sky.

SUNNY DAY

The sun is our special star, and it can always be a sunny day in your house when you make your own indoor sun. A grown-up cuts out a circle about eighteen inches in diameter from brown craft paper or cardboard. Your child then paints it yellow. When it is dry, use many different yellow and gold collage materials to decorate the sun. Add pieces of metallic gold wrapping paper to increase the sunshine. Add sun rays by drawing them in or attaching some crepe paper or yarn streamers. Hang your sun on the wall. You can also decorate both sides of your sun and hang it safely from the ceiling so that it can turn and shine all around the room.

MURAL SCENES

Think big! Murals are very large pieces of art. Young children can be busy working on a mural for several days and might enjoy making a mural with friends. Cut out a big piece of

> Accept your child's view of the world. Hair can be green, eyes can be purple, and buildings can be smaller than people.

> Your child will have her own ideas about which materials she prefers to use. Give her the opportunity to make her own choices.

craft paper about three feet wide. Tape it to the floor or wall so that it stays in place. For younger children, murals can have a general theme such as all one color or different shapes or textures. It could also be a mural based on cut-out pictures of animals, cars, buildings, foods, or children. Older children might also like to create a mural about a season, the sky, the ocean, the forest, or whatever interests them. Begin by helping your children choose the theme for their mural. They can make their mural by combining a variety of materials in different ways, painting, drawing, collaging, and printing. Gather anything and everything and lots of glue. They can add collected materials such as shells, leaves, pebbles, or whatever relates to the theme. Hang the mural on a wall and enjoy it.

When your children begin making murals, they may not cover the entire paper. Revisit mural making. As your children continue to make murals, they will become more able to make art on a larger scale.

> An easy way to use glue is to pour a small amount into a jar lid or a paper plate. Use a small paintbrush or cotton swab for gluing.

> Display your child's artwork at home. A few inexpensive picture frames of various sizes can display your family's changing "art collection." Consider having a "Picture of the Week."

PLAYING WITH PLASTICINE

Plasticine is a nonhardening modeling material that comes in a variety of colors. It offers a wonderful tactile experience for young children. They love to squeeze it, roll it, pound it, flatten it, shape it, and create with it. Plasticine does not harden and can be used over and over again for many wonderful times.

TREASURE BOXES

Save any good box that comes your way. Every child needs a treasure box or two for the little things that are important to them. Treasure boxes can hold their toy figures, pennies, stones, erasers, ticket stubs, and whatever else they collect. Sturdy boxes with tops or attached lids work well. Get out your art materials and start decorating. Make a special lining for the box by gluing fabric or paper to the inside. Treasure boxes are wonderful gifts that young children can make themselves.

PENCIL HOLDERS

Turn the cardboard roll from toilet paper into a very special pencil holder. Choose paper you like and tear it into small pieces. Tissue or lightweight wrapping paper works well. Spread the paper pieces over the bottom of a shallow pan or plastic dish. Use a brush to paint glue on the cardboard roll, covering the entire surface. Then roll the cardboard in the torn pieces of paper gradually covering its entire surface. You can wait for the glue to dry and repeat to add more or another kind of paper. Let the roll dry completely while standing on its end. Choose a base: A small box, sturdy piece of cardboard, or scrap of wood. Make a ring of glue on the base, and stand the

papered roll in the glue. Hold for a few minutes as the glue begins to set. Decorate the base however you like, painting, drawing, printing, or collage. When everything is dry, you have made a very special pencil holder.

KITCHEN MAGNETS

Hardware stores sell rolls of magnetic tape that can turn artwork into your very own set of kitchen magnets. They are simple to make, useful, and wonderful gifts. Cut cardboard from a carton, gift box, or back of a writing pad into the shape you want. Decorate however you like. For refrigerator magnets, you may want to use pictures of food. You can also draw or paint. Add a piece of magnetic tape to the back, and you have your kitchen magnet.

POCKETS

Everyone needs a pocket to hold special things, and your children can make them. Begin with a paper (not plastic or Styrofoam) plate and cut it in half. Place the two curved

When collecting materials for projects, remember that Styrofoam or plastic-coated items repel glue and paint.

edges face to face and staple them together around the edge. Tape over the staples. You have created a pocket ready for decorating. Punch a hole at the top on each side. To make a shoulder strap, attach a long piece of yarn or ribbon. To wear your pocket on your belt, attach a short piece and loop your belt through it.

ROOM SIGNS

Liven up your home with fabulous signs created by your children. They love making signs with their names for the door to their room and other places in your home. Before you know it, your children might also want to make signs that say, "Do Not Enter!" and "Private!" Begin with poster board, which is available in many colors at art and stationery stores. Cut it to a manageable size. A grownup can help with the lettering, and your child does the rest. This is a great opportunity for some "mixed media" decorating. As children get ready to read, they will recognize the words on their signs. Young children feel proud to see their signs hanging at home.

PIPE CLEANER CONSTRUCTIONS

Get ready to twist! Begin with a Styrofoam bowl and glue the bottom of the bowl to the center of a piece of cardboard, which serves as the base for your construction. Paint or color the cardboard to decorate the base. Wait for the paint and glue to dry completely. Poke some holes around the sides of the bowl. Push a pipe cleaner through each hole, and twist the end that is inside of the bowl to keep it from sliding out. Attach small, lightweight objects to the loose pipe cleaner ends outside of the bowl. These

Tape over staples and the exposed ends of pipe cleaners to avoid scratches. Masking tape works well.

Inexpensive pieces of plywood, sanded and polyurethaned, make handy, portable work boards that can then be used to set aside a "work in progress." These work boards can be stored easily in a closet or under a bed.

might include small pieces of paper, spools, buttons, fabric, and even different colored pipe cleaners twisted into interesting shapes. Experiment and explore the materials on hand to add to your construction. These pipe cleaner constructions make wonderful wall decorations with moving and dangling objects.

SHOE SCULPTURE

Artists look at everyday objects with fresh eyes. An old shoe, no longer wearable, or the leftover shoe when one is lost, can be turned into a unique three-dimensional sculpture. Explore the entire shape and every surface of the shoe. All have an inside, an outside, and a sole. Some have tongues and lace holes, zippers, elastic inserts, buckles and bows, and heels of different heights and thickness. Look at your shoe from various angles. Get out your glue, collage box, and anything and everything to decorate and build your shoe sculpture. Your child's shoe sculpture will be a special addition to your art collection. Be on the lookout for other everyday objects that can be transformed into art by your child's creativity.

MOBILES

Mobiles are fun to make and set in motion. Begin with a sturdy plastic hanger. Tie on several pieces of string, yarn, ribbon, or some of each, so that they hang down. Experiment with the length of the strings. Attach lightweight objects to the ends of each string. Consider using buttons, sections of paper towel rolls, spools, fabric scraps, or whatever you create from your collage box. Hang your mobile and watch it in motion. Mobiles can also be created with sturdy paper plates. Make holes in the center and around the rim. Put a piece of string through each hole. The string in the center will be used to hang the mobile, and the strings around the rim will hold the art. Knot and tape one end of each string to secure it to the plate. Every so often, reinvent your mobile with new artwork and a new location.

HAT MAKING

It is time to have fun making hats, and there are many ways to do it using sturdy paper plates, old baseball caps, or upside-down boxes. You can also cut a piece of flexible poster board and make a tube or cone-shaped hat by taping around the circumference. A large brown paper bag becomes a hat by rolling up the bottom into a brim. Now onto decorating your hats with "mixed media," and your children create the most marvelous hats in town. Consider a "Wear Your Own Hat," party wearing your fabulous hat collection.

BOX SCULPTURE

Boxes come in all different shapes and sizes and make great three-dimensional sculptures. Collect boxes from gifts, jewelry, cereal, spaghetti, bread crumbs, crackers, and whatever comes your way. Young children love to build with boxes, deciding how to stack and arrange them. Set out the boxes, lots of glue, and plenty of tape. Some children prefer to arrange the boxes and then glue them together. Others prefer gluing on each box as they build. You may need to wait for glue to dry before adding more boxes. Consider adding paper towel and toilet paper rolls as well as other cardboard packing materials. Older children may revisit their sculptures to add to them, decorate the many surfaces, or build a base for them. They might also enjoy building another box sculpture and connecting them together.

If there is not much art to visit first hand in your community, make a trip to the public library to look at art books for ideas and visit museum Web sites.

HAND PUPPETS

Young children are at the beginning of their puppet-making years. Paper plates, socks, brown paper lunch bags, and tongue depressors make great hand puppets. Make a face, add hair, and decorate. Your puppet might have a bowtie, earrings, hat, mustache, or glasses. For paper-plate puppets, tape on a small stick or tongue depressor as a handle. Sock puppets are worn on your child's hand. Paper bag puppets, with the face made on the bottom of the bag, are moved by your child's hand, which slides into the folded down bottom of the bag. Older children might enjoy drawing a face on the end of a tongue depressor and creating a set of easily portable puppet characters.

Art is more enjoyable if you do not have to worry about making a mess. Use a big plastic tablecloth under your art work so that you do not have to think twice about ruining a floor or carpet. It is a messy business. Dress yourself and your child accordingly, and do not worry about getting dirty—you will!

Let's Get Moving!

Give your children the basic tools to get off to a healthy start. Sedentary lifestyles and childhood obesity are putting young children's health at greater risk than ever before. Fitness for young children is vitally important, and physical activity is a must for every young child.

Build physical activity into every day. It can be as simple as dancing to music at home, walking around the block, or running in the playground. It might also be a more organized activity such as a dance class or family swim at your local community center. Now is also the time to begin talking with your children about taking care of their growing bodies. Help them understand that physical activity keeps their hearts, lungs, bones, and muscles healthy and strong.

Begin by looking at what your children are actually doing and think of ways to keep them moving. Aim for a healthy balance of activities. If your child spends a lot of time reading and drawing, get up and stretch together. If your children watch a lot of television, put on music and dance together. Add more walking to your daily routines.

Consider parking further from your destination, or getting off the bus at an earlier stop. When you get home, your children can take a run around your house or down your block before going inside.

There are many ways for young children to be physically active, and these are the years to explore them. You will be trying new activities inside and outside of your home. Some will be for your children to do on their own and others will be for the family to do together. Look for activities that are fun, recreational, and perhaps offer beginning instruction. These are often found at community centers and local neighborhood programs.

Wherever you live, whatever your schedule, find some time every day for your children to get moving. It can be as simple as walking, running, jumping, skipping, hopping, and riding a bike. Even better, get moving with them!

Remember that competition should not be the focus at this age. Keep your children active with dancing, swimming, riding bikes, walking and hiking, sports, martial arts, and playground time for running, climbing, kicking, and throwing. Over time, some children may begin to show special delight in one particular activity, which will signal you to move in that direction.

Respect your child's interests and personality. Some children are very comfortable with physical activity, and others need your encouragement to try new things. For a young child, the first time on a bike, climbing up the slide, or galloping across the dance floor may be a challenge. Physical activity helps children take risks, learn new skills, and build self-confidence. It offers a wonderful arena for creative expression and imagination as young children become soaring spaceships, flying butterflies, and climbing monkeys. As their bodies grow and change rapidly, physical activity adds to their sense of mastery and competence.

Whether in T-shirts and jeans, leotards, cleats, bathing suits, or bike helmets, every child needs to get moving. Get ready, get set, and go!

Keep in mind these important movement words:
- High and low
- Up and down
- In and out
- In front and in back
- Side to side
- Round and round
- Slow and fast
- Stop and go
- Curved and straight
- Over and under and through
- Forward and Backward
- Expand and contract
- Low and medium and high
- Big and small

These props inspire fantasy and embellish activities:
- Scarves
- Bean bags
- Instruments
- Hoops
- Blue painter's tape
- Chalk
- Beach balls
- Balloons
- Crepe paper streamers
- Carpet squares

ORGANIZED TEAM SPORTS

Organized team sports are often available for young children in local communities. Many parents consider these options that offer opportunities for structured physical activity, developing skills and self-confidence, being part of a team, and great fun.

As you think about organized team sports, be realistic about your child's readiness. Team sports can be terrific when children are enjoying the sport as well as working together with their teammates and coaches, and learning to communicate and respect each other. Keep in mind that children may not fully understand all of the rules of the game until they are seven or eight years old. Over time, they will learn to understand and play by the rules.

Team sports are not a good fit for every child. Children who love to swim do not necessarily need or want to be on a swim team with scheduled practices and meets. They may be happier swimming in a recreational, noncompetitive setting, gradually improving their skills and having fun. Organized team sports are very public events because teammates, coaches, and families are at practices and games. For many young children, this is overwhelming. It is better to wait until they are older, have more self confidence, and feel ready to join a team.

When considering organized team sports for your children, begin with some research. Find out if the team experience is more competitive or instructional. Ask who is doing the coaching and teaching and what his or her qualifications are. Attend a practice or game to see what the experience is like for the children and talk with other parents. Always make sure that the equipment being used is safe, the appropriate size for young children, and is kept in good repair.

> Young children grow and change constantly. Choose and plan physical activities that match their skills and abilities and can be done safely.

> Create a routine of stretching and moving with your child to engage his imagination. Make it fun to do together and short so that you can do it regularly.

When choosing a preschool or day care program, find out how physical activity is included and also how often. Ask what space and equipment are used and who leads these activities.

BALLOON GAMES

Balloons, both imaginary and real, can give your children a great workout, indoors or out. Warm up with an imaginary balloon that you pretend to blow up. Hold your balloon in your hands and stretch it from side to side five times. Take a deep breath, and start blowing it up. Feel your chest expand and contract. Do it again, and again, until your imaginary balloon is filled with air. Let it go and chase it as it floats away. Now you are all warmed up and ready for the real thing. Blow up a few balloons of different colors. There are many balloon games to play. Toss and catch them.

Kick one around the room or back and forth between you. Tap one against the wall and count how many taps you can do before it hits the ground. Tap one in the air. Try this to music, keeping the balloon in the air for an entire song. Make up balloon directions. "Give the red balloon a high kick, keep the yellow balloon no higher than your waist, and toss the blue balloon above your head." A package of balloons is easy to take with you wherever you go.

THE LIMBO

Grab a cardboard wrapping paper roll to use as a limbo stick, turn on some lively music, and get your muscles working! Hold one end of the stick and place the other against the wall. When friends come to play, children can hold each end of the stick. Play limbo, taking turns crawling on all fours or shimmying face up. Keep lowering the limbo stick to increase the challenge. When it is very low to the ground, switch the game to jumping over it.

If you have questions about your child's readiness for new physical activities, talk with your pediatrician, who knows your child well.

TAPE BALANCE BEAMS

Make a "balance beam" on the floor with a long piece of two-inch-wide blue painter's tape. Walk along the line one foot in front of the other. Walk with one foot on each side of the line without touching it. Walk backwards. Jump along the line. Walk on tiptoes. Walk with hands on head, shoulders, and stretched high in the air. Walk with a bean bag on your head. Walk holding a scarf in each hand high in the air. Think of other ways to balance on your beam! When you are done, pull up the tape. You can make another "balance beam" any time you want one.

TAKE A CHALK WALK

Get your chalk and prepare to draw and walk. Draw a continuous line along your sidewalk. It might go to the next house, around your block, or along the path in your local park or playground. The line can wiggle, turn a corner, zig zag, and curve. This is great to do with friends by passing the chalk from child to child. When you are done drawing, you have a very long and special chalk line. Get ready for your chalk walk. Start at one end and walk to the other. Walk back at a faster pace. Do your chalk walk while kicking a stone or paper cup along the line. Turn your chalk walk into a gallop, hop, or run. Next time, choose a different location and make your chalk walk even longer.

> Dance to all kinds of music. Dance the dances you already know and make up some new ones together.
>
> Young children become more physically coordinated during these years. You will notice significant changes in their agility and skill.

STOP AND GO

Make a red "stop" sign and a green "go" sign by coloring paper plates. Attach a handle using a tongue depressor or paper towel roll. Begin with the grownup calling out a movement direction such as hop, gallop, wiggle, or tap your knees. Everybody keeps moving until the caller holds up the red "stop" sign. Nobody moves until the caller holds up the green "go" sign. Once your children learn the game, they can take turns being the caller and sign holder.

Encourage your child to try her hardest and do her best and that will be just fine. There is no need for competition. Feeling good about physical activity is what counts.

FAMILY STRETCH

Limber up together! Each family member does a stretch and everyone else repeats it. Take turns stretching different parts of your bodies and saying what you are doing. Here are some ideas. Stretch up high to "tickle the clouds." Walk in place and "swim through the air." Do spider stretches lying on your backs with arms, legs, and fingers wiggling as you spin your webs. "Let's climb a tall ladder all the way to the top." "Let's pick fruit from the top of the tree." Stretch like a cat on your hands and knees. Sit down and row your boats. Try stretching with your eyes closed. Keep going until your family is warmed up.

BIKE RIDE TO ANYWHERE AND EVERYWHERE

Take a bike ride without leaving your house or even getting on your bike! Lie on your backs, feet up in the air. Choose your destination and start pedaling. Pedal faster, then slower. Stop for red lights. Pedal up hills and coast down. As you pedal away, talk about what you see along the road and what you will do when you get to where you are going.

Be sure to watch your children during physical activity. Keep as close as you can without hovering, especially when they are climbing.

MORNING "JOGS"

Start your days, whenever you can, with an indoor morning "jog" together without even leaving your house. This can be a short jog just to get you up and running. At home, jog in place to go on a trip to wherever your imagination takes you. You can even jog in your pajamas.

FOLLOW THE LEADER

Sometimes you move your whole body and sometimes you move one part at a time: head, shoulders, tummy, hips, arms, elbows, hands, fingers, legs, knees, feet, and toes. Take turns being the leader. The leader chooses one part of the body and does a series of movements using it. Everyone follows what the leader does and makes the same movements. This game is especially fun to play with a group of children.

FREEZE DANCING

Put on the music and start dancing. Choose music with a strong beat to make this a real workout. Stop the music, and every dancer freezes in place. Start the music, and the dancing begins. Stop the music at different intervals to make long and short dance times and keep all of the dancers on their toes. Try freezing "high" with arms up in the air and then with your whole body "low." Add tambourines, shakers, or bells to liven up the dancing. Dance with scarves in hand to get your arms moving to the beat. Freeze dancing is a great way to get moving. Try it with all kinds of music.

Some children are reluctant to try new things because they do not know what to expect. Encourage them by describing what you will be doing.

RIBBON STICKS

Watch those ribbons swirl as you get your arms moving. Ribbon sticks add color and flair to dancing and movement games. Make two ribbon sticks by taping an eight-to-ten inch piece of ribbon to the ends of two tongue depressors or cardboard rolls. Hold one ribbon stick in each hand and get your arms moving. Move them high and low, up and down, in front and in back, from side to side, and round and round. Move them down under your legs and up under your arms. Every so often, change your ribbons or add more for extra fun.

HOOP PLAY

Hoops open new possibilities to get you all moving. Look for hoops in toy stores, multipurpose stores, and catalogs. They come in two sizes and it is great to have both large and small ones. Play with hoops indoors and out. Remember to take them to the backyard, playground, or park. Music adds to hoop play, so include it whenever you can. Hoops are wonderful to use when friends come over to play. Be inventive, and your children will discover even more ways to use them. Here are some ideas to get you started:

Put your hoop on the ground and sit down inside of it. Be a seed in a flower-pot, slowly pushing through the soil, reaching up to the sun, getting taller and taller, until you are a full-size flower. Your hoop can now be an egg and you are the baby chick poking at the shell trying to get out. Next try a series of "in and out" games, playing and inventing as you go with a series of directions. Tap your hand on the ground inside of the hoop, then out. Stamp your feet outside of the hoop, then in. Put one hand and one foot outside of the hoop. Try these "in and out" games, while first clos-ing one eye and then both. Next, stand up inside your hoop. Step in and out. Jump in and out. Walk around it. Run around it. Jump around it. Create your own series of hoop movements to repeat as you play together.

Try four hands on one hoop, holding it facing each other. Move together, swinging the hoop from side to side. Raise it, lower it to the ground. Walk forwards, backwards, adding more steps as you go. Try it faster. Circle around with the hoop still in hands.

If your child is reluctant to try a new physical activity, try it again at another time without pressuring your child.

HOOPSCOTCH

Lay the hoops on the floor so that they touch each other. Jump from hoop to hoop. Older children can hop from hoop to hoop.

Add more hoops to make your "Hoopscotch" board grow.

HOOP TRAVEL

Hold a small hoop with both hands. Use it as a steering wheel as your child "drives" on a big trip, first slow, then fast, turning corners, and coming to a stop. Raise that hoop high in the air for a trip to outer space and float through the atmosphere, swerve to avoid other spaceships, twirl around the stars, and come to a slow, soft landing on the moon.

MIRROR, MIRROR

"Mirror, Mirror" is a great hoop game to play with two children. The grownup holds a large hoop upright and each child stands on one side of the hoop, looking at each other through the hoop. The hoop has become their "mirror," and the children will take turns. The first player does a movement, perhaps tapping his nose. The second player imitates what he sees in the "mirror" and copies the movement. As the first player adds to or changes the movements, the second player continues to copy what he sees in the hoop "mirror." Younger children may do one simple movement at a time. Older children might combine a few movements to make the game more challenging.

MUSICAL HOOPS

Hoops make a great "home base" for all kinds of games. Play "Musical Hoops," and when the music stops, get back inside your hoop. Scatter some hoops around, everybody runs, and when the "Stop" sign goes up, everybody jumps into a hoop.

CREPE PAPER STREAMERS

Crepe paper streamers are great fun. Have a few rolls of different colored streamers from your local party store on hand. There are many ways to use streamers when you put on music to dance or play outside. Cut long streamers for your children to hold and wave while dancing. Toss the streamers up in the air where they float until you catch them. Toss up different colored streamers and play a game by calling out which color to catch. Next, let the streamers land on the ground and call out which color to run to. Run with streamers in hand as they wave in the breeze. Dance together, each holding one end of a long streamer. Try dancing with two streamers held between you. Tear streamers into smaller pieces, toss in the air, and catch the colored "snow."

"MIMING" STORIES

Storytelling and movement go together naturally. Young children love to "mime" as stories are told in words. Everyone can be a storyteller and do the miming motions. The more details you add, the more you move, and the more fun you have.

A story can be as simple as this: "Wake up! We're yawning, stretching, opening our eyes, and jumping out of bed. We're brushing our teeth and washing our faces. Time to get dressed, open the drawer, and take out our clothes. We're pulling up our pants and pulling our shirts over our heads. Let's get on our socks and tie our shoes. Now it's time for breakfast." Tell the story and "mime" it. Tell other everyday stories about going to the supermarket, eating spaghetti, taking a bath and washing your hair, baking cookies, or playing catch.

Tell make-believe stories that you imagine and invent. Take a trip to the moon, go on an adventure walk through the jungle, search for lost treasure, or join the circus. Tell your stories over and over again, adding new details each time.

Be sure to include your child's favorite nursery rhymes and fairy tales. Be Humpty Dumpty falling off the wall. Tell the story of the "Three Little Pigs" building each house and blowing them down.

> Young children can get moving indoors as well as out. Look for physical activities to do at home so that your children stay healthy and fit.

NUMBER OF THE DAY

Pick a number from one to ten for your "Number of the Day." If your number is four, play with it throughout the day by counting your exercises in fours. Before you go out, hop four times, touch your toes four times, and twirl around four times. After lunch, take four marching steps, do four jumping jacks, and tap your knees four times. Think of more "fours" as the day goes on. You can even say good night four times.

BEACH BALLS

There is great fun playing with beach balls, and not only at the beach! They are inexpensive, easy to take with you before they are inflated, and available in a variety of sizes. Hold a beach ball in two hands over your head while you walk across a tape "balance beam." Toss a beach ball high in the air and run to catch it. Kick a beach ball back and forth between you. Play catch, tapping or throwing it. Put a beach ball in your children's hands and watch them go!

CARPET SQUARES

Carpet squares make great special spaces for games and movement. Be sure to use them on a floor or surface where they do not slide. Put several carpet squares in a row with a space between each one and jump from one to the next. Spread them out and connect them with blue painter's tape. You can spread the carpet squares randomly or in a zigzag pattern. Go from one to the next along the blue lines, moving in different ways, walking, hopping, jumping, running, crawling, or walking backwards. Try a game of "Musical Carpet Squares" as a variation on musical chairs.

SCARVES

Keep a collection of lightweight scarves on hand to use in your movement games and activities. Toss them in the air, chase them, and catch them as they float down. Try catching them with different parts of your body. Hold on to the ends of a scarf and dance together. When friends come over to play, tie several scarves together end to end. Everyone holds on along the scarf as you follow the leader, moving fast and slow, raising and lowering the scarf, and twisting in and out.

OBSTACLE COURSES

Set up an obstacle course indoors or out making sure everything is safe and manageable. Get out your hoops, tape, scarves and bean bags and add whatever other items you would like. An obstacle course for young children is a series of small movement tasks to do in a repeated sequence. Here is an example of an obstacle course: three hoops lined up on the floor to jump through one at a time, a pile of pillows to climb over, two parallel lines of blue tape on the floor to walk between, a bean bag to pick up and toss into a carton, and a carpet square to hop on. Use a piece of tape to make start and finish lines. Your children can go through an obstacle course again and again. Build an obstacle course together when friends come to play.

Science: Here, There, and Everywhere!

There is a scientist in your child ready to question, explore, observe, experiment, and discover. Great scientific adventures begin now as your child collects rocks, plants seeds, watches ice cubes float, picks up paper clips with magnets, catches fireflies, and figures out how wheels, pulleys, and gears work. Although it is unpredictable who will grow up to discover a new planet or cure the common cold, science is important for every child. Science helps children become problem solvers and creative thinkers who can bring these important skills to the significant challenges ahead.

This is the age when young children begin to ask, "Why?" and "How?" They are extraordinarily curious. Their magical thinking about how the world works slowly evolves into a more sophisticated understanding of cause and effect. They continue to ask new questions, make new observations, acquire new information, and draw new conclusions.

Sometimes their conclusions may be inaccurate and delightfully amusing. Welcome their curiosity and encourage their thinking. The right answer is not what is important at this stage. What matters most is being a young scientist in action, experimenting and observing.

Begin with the science that surrounds you, seeing it with fresh eyes. What is common knowledge to you is now new, exciting, and interesting to your child. Talk about the clouds, wind and rain, plant and animal life, what you eat and what you do not eat, cars and trucks, the sun, moon, and stars, and your child's own growing body. You do not have to have all of the answers. It can be great fun to learn with your child through observation, hands-on activities, and a bit of research in your local library or on the Web. Remember, during your scientific adventures together that it is important to help your child develop a lasting respect for nature and the environment.

So sharpen your senses, grab your magnifying glass, and off you go discovering that science is here, there, and everywhere!

Books add to your scientific knowledge. Many wonderful storybooks illustrate changes in nature and animal life. Remember to look at nonfiction books as well.

Equip your young scientist by gradually accumulating a few tools of the trade. Your children will be excited as they use them to explore.

- Magnifying glasses
- Magnets—bar and horseshoe
- Small plastic animal tanks or fish tanks
- Sealable plastic bags for collecting
- Measuring tools—rulers, yardsticks, measuring tapes, measuring cups
- Ping-pong balls
- Flashlights

"LOOKING UP" WALK

Do not miss out on all there is to see when you look up! Instead of looking straight ahead or down at your feet, go for a walk holding your child's hand for safety while she looks up. Talk about what you see. Try this at different times of day, when the weather changes, and in various seasons. There is so much to observe. Clouds have different forms and colors. Learn their different names and what weather each brings. Notice where the sun is at different times of the day. Watch the moon pass through its phases and the stars coming out at night. Take a "Looking Up" walk in a park or wooded area. Look up at trees while standing underneath the branches. Take "Looking Up" walks regularly. You will always see something interesting and beautiful. Remember to try a "Looking Down" walk as well!

"NO RECIPE" PLAY DOUGH

If your children have used and made play dough and know what it is, try having them make it without a recipe to follow. Put out flour, salt, and water. Give your child a large mixing bowl but no measuring cups. The challenge is to use these ingredients to make play dough through experimentation, trial and error. Your child will figure out what needs to be added to make usable play dough. More water? More flour? More salt? Keep trying until a usable play dough is made. Roll up your sleeves and dig in! Revisit this activity from time to time to see if making "No Recipe" play dough gets easier.

COLORED ICE CUBES

Mix food coloring in water and fill an ice cube tray to make colored ice cubes. When the ice cubes are frozen, put one in a glass of

Visit zoos, aquariums, botanical gardens, planetariums, and natural history museums. Also consider destinations such as pet stores, local lakes and ponds, waterfalls, backyards, rock formations, parks, dairies, and farms.

clear water and watch what happens. Time how long it takes for the ice cube to melt. Melt another ice cube in hot water and time that as well. Try it with two ice cubes in the same container. Try melting a colored cube in a smaller amount of water. Make different colored ice cubes and melt them in the same container of water. What happens when you melt a blue and a red ice cube in the same water? Try this in different ways and observe what happens.

When you are out in the park or the woods, be respectful of the natural environment. When you look under a rock or find a nest, leave them as you found them to preserve the animal and plant life living there.

WATCHING YOURSELF GROW

Your children are very aware of being little and that they are always growing. In addition to marking their heights on the wall, here is a way for them to see that they are really growing over time. Use sturdy paper or cardboard and trace your child's hands and bare feet. Cut them out and label with the date. Make another traced set of hands and feet a few months later and observe any changes. Repeat

every so often and see what happens. Over time, your children will see that their hands and feet have actually gotten bigger.

Make a full-body tracing using a roll of brown craft paper. While your child lies down flat on the paper, trace the outline of his body. Cut out the shape and measure it from head to toe. Children love to paint or "dress" these figures and have a life-size replica of themselves. Repeat this activity when some "growing time" has passed and your child can observe and measure how much he has grown.

FREEZING AND HEATING

In their everyday lives, your children have seen what happens when heat and cold are used. Now try some science by applying heat and cold. Take an apple and cut it in half. Put one half in the freezer and one in a hot oven. Observe what happens. Try the same thing with a lettuce leaf, dried cereal, chocolate, water, or whatever you think might be interesting. Grownups will have to use the knife and the oven.

FIZZ, FIZZ, FIZZ!

See chemistry in action. Combine vinegar and baking soda and observe the results. Fill a small plastic measuring cup with white vinegar. Give your child a large metal mixing bowl. Have her begin by pouring in some baking soda, perhaps a few tablespoons. Then have her pour in the vinegar a little at a time. Observe what happens. Add more vinegar, more baking soda, and watch what happens every time you add something. You can also put a few drops of food coloring in the vinegar for variety. Because this is messy if it overflows, you may want to set the bowl in your sink before you begin.

CAPILLARY ACTION IN ACTION

All living things need water. Your children can see how water travels through a plant to help it survive. Make a solution of colored water with food coloring. Take a stalk of celery with the leaves still on and make a fresh cut across

Learn what you need to know to do science activities with your children by reading a short book written specifically for children. These books include the most important information presented in a simple, direct style, and give you the basic information easily and quickly.

the bottom. Look at the small holes in the stalk. These are the veins of the plant. Stand the celery in the water solution. Watch what happens over the next few hours as the celery drinks up the water through its veins. Try this with different colored solutions, stalks of different lengths, and a stalk without leaves. Leave a stalk of celery out of water for several days and compare the two.

OIL AND WATER

Solutions are an important part of chemistry. See what happens when you try to mix oil and water. Use a clear plastic jar with a lid that can be screwed on tightly. Pour in three inches of salad oil. Add a few drops of food coloring to water and pour a few inches of this solution into the jar. Watch what happens. Put on the lid tightly and shake the jar vigorously. Let the solution settle and see how it ends up. Repeat and observe the results. Add different liquids to see what happens.

PLANT YOUR LUNCH

Start collecting the seeds from the food you eat. Include orange, lemon, apple, grapefruit, tomatoes, pepper, and watermelon seeds. Also save pits from peaches, plums, avocados, and cherries. Keep your eyes open for other fruits and vegetables that have seeds or pits. Examine what you have collected. Cut open a few seeds and pits to see what is inside. Try different ways of growing seeds. Place some seeds on a wet paper towel and moisten daily. Plant a few seeds in water and others in soil. See what happens and be prepared for a variety of results. Older children may want to keep a log or chart of what they observe.

Science is not always a project to do. It is all around you—water boiling and freezing, children growing taller, bananas turning brown, and the sun rising and setting.

SURE TO GROW

Some seeds are almost certain to sprout and grow quickly. Use marigold and radish seeds, which are available in markets and plant centers. Fill a clear plastic cup with soil, sprinkle in some seeds, and add a bit of water every day. Observe what happens. Your children can keep a record of what they see each day.

POTATO PLANTS

This great favorite is a wonderful activity for young children. Take a sweet or white potato and insert toothpicks around the middle. Place it in a transparent container of water so that the toothpicks rest on the edge of the container. The bottom of the potato sits in the water. Add more water as needed to keep the bottom of the potato wet. Observe the changes as leaves sprout and the roots grow down into the water. Be sure to observe what happens to the potato as it grows into a plant. Older children might want to draw the changes they observe.

Your science observations and knowledge will be enhanced with a basic home collection of nature guide books. These will be useful as you explore, learn about, and identify trees, leaves, flowers, insects, rocks, and shells.

HERB AND GREENHOUSE TERRARIUMS

Terrariums are closed sealed containers used to grow and observe plant life. You can make a terrarium together and grow your own herbs. Use a very large clear plastic container from a gallon of water or a two-liter beverage bottle. Make sure to keep the cap on. Cut the container so that the bottom part is at least three inches high. Fill the bottom with two inches of soil and plant some herb seeds. Parsley and chives work well. Water the seeds. Tape the parts of the container back together using clear plastic tape. Keep the cap tightly sealed so that your terrarium is a closed system. Remove the cap only to water the seeds as needed. Enjoy your terrarium herbs when you cook together.

You can also build a greenhouse terrarium in the same way. Take a walk to gather rocks, moss, twigs, and small plants. Add them to the terrarium. Water and seal tightly. Over time, observe how the water evaporates, condenses, and recycles to water the plants. Your terrarium is actually a greenhouse.

LEAF COLLECTIONS

Young children find leaves interesting and love to pick them up and have a closer look. Be scientists when you collect leaves with your children, noting where you found each leaf and the date. This will be useful information so you can revisit the same location at different times of the year and

Egg cartons make great indoor gardens for planting seeds. Each compartment can hold a different kind of seed or you can test out various watering conditions in each one. When your plants get bigger, transplant them to flower pots, window boxes, or your garden.

observe leaf changes. When you collect leaves with your children, take out your magnifying glass and look closely. Learn the names of the leaf parts and trace the vein system with your fingers. Observe color, shape, texture, and how the stem is attached to the branch. Talk about why leaves are important and what role they play in keeping trees alive.

Start a "Leaf Book" in a loose-leaf binder and add leaves as your collection grows. Glue each leaf to paper, cover with clear contact paper, and add to your binder. Look at a tree guide to identify the leaves, adding the name to each page.

DOES EVERYTHING GROW?

Try this variation on planting seeds to help your children begin to differentiate between living and nonliving things: Collect some easy-to-grow seeds such as marigolds or radishes, a plastic bottle cap, a sheet of paper, and some other small inanimate objects. Plant them all in a large container. Label where each object is planted. Water, predict what will happen, and observe the results. This experiment helps you talk about living and nonliving things.

> Give your children their own plants. Choose one that is easy to care for and sure to grow. Keeping a plant alive and observing it closely is daily science at home.

ADOPT A TREE

Your children can choose a tree on your block, in your neighborhood, backyard, local park, or nature preserve. They will be learning about their trees in many ways. Start by learning the basics. Find out the name of your tree. Draw it and take a photo of it. Note its location and what other types of trees and plants are nearby. Feel its bark and make a bark rubbing. Look under your tree for seed pods, leaves, and small fallen branches to examine. Observe the ground around your tree to see if any roots are visible and follow them out from the tree to see how far they go. Use a piece of string to measure around your tree. This is your tree's circumference. Keep a close watch for any signs of animals who live in, under, or at the top of your tree. Always have your magnifying glass with you to take a closer look.

Visit your tree from time to time, especially as the seasons and weather vary, to observe any changes. When you continue this activity over time, your children will learn more about growth, change, and the environment. Everyone in your family, grownups included, can adopt a tree.

Older children may want to keep a "Tree Journal" to record their observations and keep their collection of photographs, drawings, leaves, seeds, and bark.

> When you set out to do science activities, leave room for experimentation and discovery. Expect the unexpected.

FLOATING AND SINKING

Your bathtub, kitchen sink, or a large plastic bin turns into a science laboratory for experiments with floating and sinking. Your child begins by collecting some small waterproof objects such as a crayon, ball, wooden block, plastic toy, or cup. First, predict what will happen and then place each object in the water one by one. Observe which ones sink and which stay afloat. You can also observe which take longer to sink.

Add some new objects to your experiment and make predictions before placing each one in the water.

Next, or another time, find a small plastic container that will float and place it on top of the water like a boat. Put different small objects, one by one, in your "boat" to see what it can hold and still float. Paper clips, marbles, or ping-pong balls work well because you can count how many it takes before your boat sinks. Aluminum foil can also be shaped into a small boat that your children can float on water to discover how much it can hold before sinking.

This activity can be repeated many times, varying the depth of the water, the size and shape of the containers, and the objects used to float or sink. Try the same activities with salt water.

MAGNETS

Discovering the power of magnets is exciting for young children. This science in action looks like magic. You may have a magnet holding papers on your refrigerator. Start there to observe how magnets work. Will the magnet attach to a wooden or plastic surface, or to the wall? Next, move on to bar and horseshoe magnets, which are available at toy and hardware stores. Your children can experiment to see what their magnets pick up or stick to. Can the magnet attract through paper? Water? Wood? Put a few paper clips in a small sturdy glass jar. Will the magnet pull the paper clips up the side of the jar? Discover what happens when you hold two magnets near each other. Magnets are always interesting and fun to use, so keep them available for your children to revisit.

DISSECTING FLOWERS

Flowers are beautiful and a great example of how nature works. When you are out walking, always stop to notice the flowers along the way, observing the shapes, colors, stems, leaves, and petals. Choose a flower to bring home and take apart. Look at the whole flower first, its different parts and how they are all connected. Then take it apart. Dissect the flower and look closely at each part with your magnifying glass. Learn the scientific name of each part and what it does for the flower: pistil, stamen, petal, pollen, leaf, stem. Gently crush the flower parts with your fingers to see what they feel like and if they are moist. When you are done, set your flower parts aside and look at them in a day or two. How have they changed?

Your children can use art materials to make some flowers, now that they know the parts to include. They can make their flowers with pipe cleaners, paper, tissue, and even use some of the dried petals from the flowers they dissected.

These are the years to begin saying, "Let's look it up!" Your local library and the Internet are great resources for your family to use.

Wooden tongue depressors are a terrific addition to your supplies. They are available at pharmacies and craft stores. Keep a supply on hand for using in art, science, and cooking.

INCLINED PLANES

You can have a great time building a ramp and watching gravity and momentum in action. To construct the ramp, take a few cereal boxes or pieces of firm carton cardboard and tape them together. A long piece of plywood also works well. Lean your ramp against a sturdy support such as a wall or a piece of furniture. This ramp is actually an inclined plane. Gather an assortment of objects such as miniature cars, crayons, different sized balls, and blocks. Begin at the top of the ramp, and one by one, release each object and observe what happens. Make predictions about how fast and how far each object will go and which may not move at all. Try other objects including some that are not round and some that are heavier. Release two objects at the same time and predict which will reach the bottom first and which will go further. Change the angle of your inclined plane or make it longer. See what happens to the speed and distance of the objects as you release them. Older children may want to measure how far the objects have rolled using colored yarn or string. Experiment, revisit this activity, and let the good times roll.

BOUNCING, BOUNCING, BOUNCING!

A ball is one of the first toys for young children. Your children can use them in different ways to learn about gravity. You can use tennis balls, beach balls, rubber spaldings, ping-pong balls, and other balls of various sizes. Hold two of the same kind, or two different balls, and drop them from the same height at the same time. Observe how high they bounce and count how many times they bounce. What happens if you release them from higher or lower? Roll the balls off of the edge of a table, one at time, then two of the same, and then two different ones. Observe the bouncing. Try bouncing the balls on different surfaces such as sidewalks, grass, or dirt. Older children might want to measure and chart how high and how many times each ball bounces.

Earthworms are interesting to observe. When you are out walking, look for them under rocks. You will also see more of them after a big rain.

GIVE YOURSELF A HAND!

Young children use their hands all the time and now can take a scientific look at both the inside and outside of hands. Begin with a close observation of both your hands. Feel the elasticity of skin when you pinch it. Look at your veins and feel your bones through your skin. Tap your fingernails to observe how they are different than skin. Open and close your hands to feel the muscles at work. Now you are ready to construct a model of a hand from the inside out.

Trace an adult hand on cardboard. Cut it out to make the "bones" of your hand. Make a layer of "muscles" with plasticine or play dough and place it on the bones. Use pipe cleaners to make "veins" and place them on the muscle layer. Your bones, muscles, and veins are covered with skin. Cover the model of your hand with "skin" by sliding it into a clear plastic glove from the drugstore. Cut "fingernails" from construction paper and glue them in place. Your model hand now has all of the parts you have observed on your own hand, both inside and out.

If you are unsure how an activity will work, try it on your own without your child for a trial run.

STRING SLIDES

Take several yards of string and a paper cup and you are set to see gravity at work. Poke a hole in the bottom of the cup and put the string through it. Tie the ends of the string to two chairs so that it is suspended parallel to the floor. How can you make the cup move along the string? Move it with your finger or blow into it to create wind to propel it. This takes work and energy from you. Next, retie the string so that it is at an angle, one end higher than the other. Slide your cup to the top and observe what happens when you let go. How much work or energy did it take to get the cup moving? Experiment with different sizes and types of cups and vary the angle of the string. Try using the spools from thread or the inside rolls of ribbon. Predict and observe the results.

COLLECTING ROCKS

Pebbles, stones, and rocks are everywhere. Young children love to pick them up, feel them, hold them, and bring them home. This beginning geology is great fun. Take a magnifying glass and a container and collect wher-ever you are. Your child can begin a rock jour-nal to note where each rock was found and its environment. Observe your rocks closely and notice the color, streaks, luster, and surface. Wash your rocks and re-examine the surface. Look in a rock guide book to identify and classify the rocks. Your child can sort and group rocks by color, where they were found, or type.

Observation is an important part of science. When you do sci-ence activities, observe along with your children to enjoy what you see together.

WHERE DO PUDDLES GO?

Young children love to jump in puddles and often notice when these puddles get smaller and smaller and finally disappear. Your children can experiment with evaporation at home. Fill several containers of various diameters with an inch of water. Place the containers near a window. Look at them daily. Now try using the same size containers and put them in different places. What happens? Try this with heavily salted water and observe the results.

SPROUTING BEANS

Dried beans sprout quickly, and your children can observe this process. Line a clear plastic container or jar with damp paper towels. Place the dried beans between the wet towels and the side of the jar so that you can see them. Add a small amount of water each day to the bottom of the jar, keeping it sealed. Observe the germination process and the new plant that emerges from the bean.

SHADOWS

A small magnifying glass is great to have with you when you are exploring the outdoors.

Shadows fascinate young children as they discover and play with them. When they observe shadows, they are learning that light does not pass through solid objects. Outdoors, the sun provides the light and your children are the solid objects. On a sunny day, go to the same place at different times of the day. What happens to your children's shadows as they move around? Can they make their shadows longer and shorter? Can they make their shadows longer than yours? Do they always have a shadow? Can they leave their shadows behind? Can they jump into your shadow without jumping into you? When you are outdoors, observe the shadows of trees, plants, buildings, cars, and people walking down the street.

It is great fun to use chalk to trace your shadows on the sidewalk. On a sunny day, choose a spot and trace your child's shadow.

A few hours later, stand in the same spot and trace your child's shadow again. Compare the tracings and observe the changes.

Make shadows indoors by using a flashlight. Your child now provides the light by focusing the flashlight on solid objects and observing the shadows. Your children can shine the light on their hands to make shadows on the walls. Hold the flashlight for them as they wiggle and dance and make a shadow show.

There Is Music in the Air!

Wherever there are young children, you will hear music. Tapping rhythms on the kitchen table, singing to themselves while they draw, listening to favorite songs in the car, or making up a march on the playground, children and music come together naturally. Every culture has lullabies, nursery rhymes, and games that bring music into a child's life from the very beginning. Your child's experience with music grows as you listen to music together and share favorite songs.

No matter how you bring music into your children's lives, you are building on a foundation that is already in place. You do not need a formal background in music. To enrich their experience, go beyond what is written specifically for young children. They may enjoy jazz, classical, show tunes, rock, folk, country, and music from all over the world. You never know what will spark your child's enthusiasm and interest. Be sure to include the music that you love best. Your enjoyment will be contagious.

All kinds of music is the best music! Listen to music you love, not only music written for children. Jazz, classical, folk, rock, show tunes—all can be enjoyed by your children and you together.

Music calls for spontaneity. You can make music anytime because the basic tools are always with you. Sing, whistle, hum, tap out rhythms, and move to the beat wherever you are. Consider music for all sorts of family times. Sing your way through traffic jams or while cooking dinner. Create your own music as needed, such as an "Anti-monster Chant" or a "Taking off the Band-Aid" rap. Enjoy these homemade musical treasures as they become part of your family's repertoire.

There are many ways to make music with your children. What matters most is having fun together and filling the air with music.

ABOUT MUSIC LESSONS

Some young children begin to show a talent or special interest in music, and you may consider private lessons. Look for a

84

Expand your family's listening "repertoire" to music from different places. Music from around the world sung by children is a wonderful way to begin your travels and learn about other cultures.

teacher who works well with young children and knows how to make the lessons enjoyable. To find a teacher, talk with other parents, early childhood teachers, and the music school in your community. Some music teachers encourage parents to stay during the lesson. This gives parents the chance to see the teacher's style and how your child responds. Parents can also see if their children are enjoying the lessons. Most young children begin private lessons with piano or violin because these instruments are best suited for their age. Lessons go well when kept short. Some children love music but may not be ready for private music lessons until they are older. Continue enjoying music together until they are ready.

VISITING THE INSTRUMENTS

Find out where musical instruments are sold in your community. It might be a specialized store devoted solely to instruments or a section of a larger, multipurpose store. Take a music trip to visit the instruments. This is a great way to learn the names of the instruments and see their different sizes, shapes, and what they are made of. If there is a salesperson available, perhaps you can hear the sounds of the different instruments, touch them, and see how the sounds are produced.

HEARING LIVE MUSIC

Look for opportunities for your child to see and hear live music played. Perhaps you can visit a friend who plays an instrument. Be open to other opportunities as well. School marching bands and choruses, local high school concerts and "battles of the bands," and public library performances are wonderful ways for young children to hear live music. Open rehearsals may be available in your community and are great for young children because you can stay for a short time. You may also know a teenager who plays an instrument who can visit with her instrument and spend some music time with your child.

FAMILY SING

Set aside a time when your family gets together and everyone comes ready to sing a favorite song or two. Share your songs, gradually learning everybody's favorites and adding new ones each time. Include the songs of even your youngest children. You might also plan this activity for a family holiday get together. Family Sings with another family are fun and you learn each other's favorites. Add to your Family Sing with instruments, clapping, and singing rounds.

Ask grandparents and great-grandparents to share the songs they sang when they were children. Some of these songs may be from wherever your family originated. Your children can learn "old" family favorites from another time and place.

BECOME A RECORDING ARTIST

Children enjoy hearing their own voices. Record their singing and music making. Choose a few songs to practice. Keep adding songs to the recording every so often for a big family hit. A recording of your children's singing and music making is a great gift for the people who love them.

BECOME A SONGWRITER

When you discover a piece of instrumental music that your children enjoy, make up words together to the melody. Be inventive and experiment with different kinds of music. Include nonsense words and sounds. Sometimes it helps to get started by singing to a familiar melody that everyone knows such as "Twinkle, Twinkle Little Star."

RHYTHM GAMES

Improvise together! Clapping and tapping rhythms is music in the making. Sitting or standing, indoors or out, get your hands and feet moving. One person begins by tapping or clapping a simple rhythm and everyone repeats it. Keep the game going, taking turns. Change the rhythms adding new beats each time. Tap softer, louder, faster, slower. Tap on your knees, your head, your hips, your shoulders, and the floor. Use your voices to add words and sounds. Snap your fingers and get the rhythm going.

Help your children learn how to be in an audience at a performance. Children are ready to be part of an audience when they are able to sit quietly while listening and paying attention to the performance. Readiness varies with age, interest, and personality. Look for concerts and musical events for children that are engaging, fun, and less than an hour long. Before you go, talk about what they will see and hear and try to listen to the music. After the performance, talk about what you have seen and heard. Your children will enjoy these experiences and so will you.

HOLIDAY SONGS

Some holidays and family get-togethers lend themselves to music. Music and singing can become lively parts of your family's holiday traditions. As a holiday approaches, choose a few songs to sing together in preparation. You might have favorites that you want to pass on to your children and they might have some new songs to share with you. When the holiday actually arrives, your children will be ready to join in when everyone sings together. Your children may also have a special new song that they would like to share with the family. Consider bringing song sheets so that everyone can sing along with them as a new family tradition is created.

BE THE CONDUCTOR

Young children make great conductors! They love to conduct any kind of music with their arms and imaginations. Turn up the music so that it fills the room and let the conducting begin. This is a great time to listen to really robust symphonic music with lots of instruments and even a chorus joining in. Create a make-believe "podium" for your maestro and let the music begin.

FOLLOW THE BEAT

You have probably found yourself tapping your fingers or feet when listening to music. Your children can join in. Listen to some music you enjoy together and follow the beat. Tap it out together. Use hands, feet, and a big wooden spoon on a plastic container. Vary the music as you vary the beat.

SHEET MUSIC COLLAGE

Music has its own written language filled with notes, lines, and many different symbols. You can find some written music in the library or in a book and make copies to look at together. Then cut it up into shapes to make a music collage. You can also use these music pages to cover the containers or boxes for your CDs and instruments. A music collage is a great gift for someone who especially loves music.

Kazoos and bells are great additions to your children's instrument collection. Consider getting a kazoo for every member of your family (grownups included).

HOMEMADE INSTRUMENTS

People all over the world have been making their own instruments for thousands of years. Your children can join in this tradition. Be creative as you make your own percussion instruments for music making. You might enjoy looking at pictures of instruments from other times and places in books or on the Web as you become instrument makers.

DRUMS

There are many ways to make drums using different objects. Every object will produce its own sound when it becomes a drum. Begin with a cylindrical oatmeal box or coffee can, making sure there are no sharp edges on the can. Leave the lid on your drum. Cut a piece of contact paper to fit around your drum and leave on the backing. Decorate the front of the contact paper with stickers and flat collage materials. Peel off the backing and attach the decorated contact paper around your drum.

Different-shaped drums can be made the same way using a heavy-duty cardboard roll from wrapping paper or mailing tubes, which come in different lengths. Each will produce its own sound. Play them either flat on the floor or by standing them upright.

There may be opportunities to hear music from other cultures performed in your local community. This is a great way to introduce music from around the world to your children.

Make a set of drums using a collection of different sized small, sturdy cardboard boxes. Secure the lids, decorate them, and glue them onto a large piece of cardboard to make a portable drum set.

Drumsticks that are safe, light, and that fit your children's hands can be found around your house. Try wooden spoons, chopsticks, or unsharpened pencils. Make a different sound on your drum by using various sized paint or pastry brushes to play them.

SHAKERS

A collection of shakers adds to the beat when you make music. Small, clear, plastic water bottles with tight fitting tops as well as small metal candy tins two to four inches in diameter can be turned into shakers. Fill them with dried beans, small pebbles, buttons, or paper clips. Make sure you secure the top. Each combination of containers and what you put inside will produce a unique sound.

TAMBOURINES

Paper plates with a slight lip or rim work best to make a tambourine. Staple them together, front to front, and fill them with dried beans before stapling it completely. Tape around the edge to cover the staples. Add some ribbon streamers and if you have them, some bells. Decorate your tambourine.

SPOON CHIMES

Spoons can also make music. Collect four or five different spoons and a plastic hanger. Use string to hang the spoons from the hanger by tying one end to the spoon and one end to the hanger. Attach them right-side-up or upside-down, depending on the shape of the spoons. Leave a few inches between each spoon. The spoons should hang at about the same level with enough distance between them so that they can swing and tap each other. Use another spoon to play your chimes by tapping the hanging spoons and get them swinging.

SANDPAPER BLOCKS

Another handy instrument for your collection is sandpaper blocks. Take two matching blocks and trace their shape onto coarse sandpaper. A grownup will need to cut out the sandpaper pieces. Glue the sandpaper onto each block. When they dry, rub the coarse sandpaper surfaces together to make a new sound. If you do not have blocks, use two small sturdy boxes or small round tins that fit into your child's hand.

I HEAR A PARADE!

It is time to get up and march to the beat. Put on some marching music that gets you up on your feet. Grab your instruments. Drum a small pot with a kitchen spoon, toot your paper towel roll horn, or bang your wooden-spoon rhythm sticks. March around a room, down the hall, into the kitchen, and wherever your marching feet lead you. Take turns being the head of the parade.

Be open to moments when you can play-fully sing a song you know or create one for what you are doing. Your own "Sorting the Socks" or "Walking Around the Block" songs are sure to become family favorites! Begin with a familiar tune you know or make up your own.

Look Who's Cooking!

Put on your aprons and into the kitchen you go! Cooking with your children can be great fun, a wonderful learning experience, and a genuine help in preparing food for your family. It is a great activity to do with any number of children. You do not have to be a master chef to give it a try. Without a doubt, cooking with children requires extra preparation and cleanup, and the results may not always be what you expect. There are many terrific times ahead when you roll up your sleeves, grab your wooden spoons, and get cooking.

Even though cooking requires more adult direction and supervision than many other activities, young children can be active participants rather than extra company in the kitchen watching you cook. Look for recipes with tasks that children can do. Invest in some basic cooking equipment that they can use safely and comfortably, including child-sized wooden spoons, rolling pins, whisks, and mini-graters. Metal bowls, plastic measuring cups, nonserrated butter knives, mini-muffin tins, small loaf pans, and a child-sized apron are also great additions. Choose a work space that your child can reach, either a kitchen table or a counter using a safe, steady stool.

Cooking together begins the conversation about food, nutrition, and healthy eating. These are important topics for all parents. Cooking together offers opportunities for children to try new foods and many different ways to prepare them. Young children also learn about different food groups and begin to understand what their growing bodies need to be healthy and strong. While chopping and mixing, you can be chatting away about which foods you need every day, which are for once in awhile, and which are for special occasions.

When you cook together, talk about what you are doing. Your child is learning all the time from organizing and categorizing foods, following the sequence of a recipe, measuring ingredients, and observing what

> While cooking together with your children, you may recall your own childhood memories of being in the kitchen. Share these important and meaningful memories.

happens when you stir and mix, and use heat and cold in your "kitchen chemistry." Firsthand experience gives special meaning to the names of foods, utensils, and cooking terms. Teaspoon, tablespoon, cup, pint, quart, liter, half, quarter, pound, sift, stir, fold, beat, spread, crushed, ripe, pinch, combine, knead, melt, garnish, oblong, square, loaf, layer, ingredients, blanch, yeast, dough, batter, chopped, grated, sprinkle, optional, topping, seasoning, spices, flatten, and shredded all become part of your child's expanding vocabulary.

It is a wonderful experience for young children to prepare food and then share it with their families. The pride your children feel when everybody takes a first taste is extraordinary. Children know they have really contributed to the family table. Cooking is also a way to share meaningful traditions and memories. Making old family recipes or what you enjoyed as a child helps connect your children to their roots. Time in the kitchen with grandparents, other family members, and close friends also builds these connections.

Safety is always first! Your children need to know from the beginning that you are completely in charge of the stove, microwave, and all other electrical appliances. Do not use sharp knives around children. Prepare ingredients that require cutting with sharp knives in advance. Avoid using glass containers or tools with breakable and sharp parts. Substitute plastic or disposable aluminum pans whenever possible. Always handle hot baking dishes, pots, pans, and micro-waved foods yourself and keep them away from your children.

Choose a recipe and get cooking. Remember that it does not matter if the cake caves in or the bread does not rise. It is the "doing" and having a good time together that matters the most.

> Take a trip to the supermarket together after you have chosen your recipe and you are getting ready to cook. As you look for ingredients, talk about how they are organized by food groups in the market. It is fun to find butter, flour, eggs, zucchini, apples, and spices each in their own special place.

RECIPES YOU DON'T HAVE TO COOK!

No need to turn on the stove to have a good time preparing food with your children! Make these simple recipes together for a snack or a meal.

Ants on a Log

Spoon cream cheese, cottage cheese, or peanut butter onto four-inch pieces of celery. Add raisins along the center of the "logs."

Salad to Go

Start with a flat-bottomed ice cream cone. Put a few small pieces of lettuce in the bottom of the cone, add a scoop of cottage cheese, and top it with small cut pieces of fruit or vegetables. Try some crushed pineapple for a refreshing treat.

Red, White, and Blue Parfait

Spoon an inch of vanilla yogurt into a clear plastic cup. Add a layer of sliced strawberries and another layer of yogurt. Add a layer of blueberries and more yogurt. Repeat the layers until you get to the top. A topping of granola gives your parfait some crunch.

Fruit Kabobs

For skewers, use sturdy plastic coffee stirrers or wooden kabob sticks with the sharp ends cut off. Cut fruits such as apples, bananas, pineapples, strawberries, and grapes into pieces. Push the fruit pieces onto the skewers.

Washing hands thoroughly with soap is the first step when you prepare food. Make sure this gets done each and every time.

Rice Cake Faces

Spread a rice cake with peanut butter or cream cheese. Use raisins and pieces of fruit to design a face.

Snacklaces

Take a full strand of red shoestring licorice and make a knot in one end. String mini-pretzels and doughnut shaped cold cereals on the licorice. Tie the ends together. Wear it as a necklace and snack on it bit by bit.

There is a lot of math in cooking. Give your children hands-on experience using a set of graduated measuring cups and spoons. These clearly show what third, quarter, half, and whole actually mean. Using these terms as you measure helps your children begin to understand these important math concepts.

Hot Dog Roll
Banana Sandwiches

Spread a hot dog roll with peanut butter or cream cheese. Slip a whole banana into the roll. Add raisins, nuts, chocolate or carob chips, honey, or granola as you like.

Paper-Cup
Popsicles

Pour orange or other fruit juice in small paper cups. Place in freezer. When they are slightly frozen, add a tongue depressor as a handle. Put back in the freezer until completely frozen. To eat, run under warm water for a moment and the popsicle will slide out of the cup.

Food Creature Faces

Place a scoop of tuna salad, chicken salad, mashed potatoes, or cottage cheese in the middle of a large plate and flatten slightly with the back of a spoon. Design your creature's features with string bean antennae, cucumber nose, alfalfa sprout hair, cherry tomato eyes, a red pepper mouth, and a celery stick neck. Create your creature with whatever you have on hand and try a fruit version as well.

Children need help learning how to crack an egg. Show your child how to give the egg three taps on the side of a bowl, the last tap being the hardest. Show her how to put both thumbs in the crack and pull apart the two halves of the shell so that the egg slides out. It takes practice! And do not forget to hold the egg over the bowl.

Apple Bread Pudding

This pudding makes a nutritious breakfast as well as a delicious snack or dessert. Serve it cold or warm from the oven. Experiment using different kinds of bread or whatever you have on hand. Tearing bread, beating eggs, and measuring ingredients give children plenty to do.

4 beaten eggs

2 cups milk

⅓ cup sugar

½ teaspoon ground
   cinnamon

½ teaspoon vanilla

3 cups of bread torn
   into one inch pieces

1 apple, peeled and
   chopped

⅓ cup raisins (optional)

1. Preheat oven to 325° F.
2. Beat together eggs, milk, sugar, cinnamon, and vanilla.
3. Grease a small baking dish or loaf pan.
4. Place bread pieces, apples, and raisins in the greased baking dish.

5. Pour egg mixture over the bread mixture.
6. Sprinkle a mixture of cinnamon and sugar on top if you like.
7. Bake 45 minutes, or until a knife inserted near the center comes out clean.
8. Serve warm or cool.

Apple Crisp

Munching apple peels and slices along the way, this easy recipe will be great fun to make together for a family dessert. Plastic knives can be used to slice the apples and a big wooden spoon is just right for mixing the topping. Remember that perfect apple slices are not important at all. It will taste great no matter how you slice it!

4 cups peeled
   and sliced (about 4
   medium) apples

⅔ to ¾ cup packed brown sugar

½ cup unbleached flour

½ cup oats

¾ teaspoon cinnamon

¾ teaspoon nutmeg

⅓ cup margarine
   or butter, softened

When your children and their friends are cooking with you, remember to divide the recipe into smaller pans so that every child has a dish to take home. Keep a variety of disposable aluminum loaf and muffin pans on hand for these occasions.

1. Preheat oven to 375° F.
2. Grease an 8-by-8 pan or pie plate.
3. Spread the sliced apples in the baking pan.
4. Mix the remaining ingredients completely and sprinkle the mixture over the sliced apples.
5. Bake 20 to 30 minutes until the topping is golden brown and the apples are tender.

Applesauce or Pumpkin Bread

Here is a great recipe for your children to make with either pumpkin or applesauce. You can adjust the spices and sweetness to suit your family's taste. Be sure to enjoy the aroma of the spices when adding them and watch what happens when dry and wet ingredients combine.

2 eggs

¼ cup water

⅓ vegetable oil

1 cup canned unsweetened pumpkin
    or 1 cup applesauce

½ teaspoon cinnamon

¼ teaspoon nutmeg

Pinch of mace or ground cloves

1⅓ cups unbleached flour

½ teaspoon salt

2 teaspoons baking soda

1¼ cups sugar or ¾ cups maple syrup

1. Preheat oven to 350° F.
2. In a large bowl, mix eggs, water, oil, pumpkin or applesauce, and the spices.
3. In a separate bowl, mix the flour, salt, baking soda, and sugar together.
4. Pour the dry ingredients into the wet and combine thoroughly.
5. Pour batter into greased loaf pans.
6. Bake 1 hour if making a larger 9-by-5 loaf or for ½ to ¾ hour if using smaller-size pans.

Banana Bread

Make this easy, nutritious recipe to have a delicious breakfast or snack. You can also add some chocolate chips for variety. Bake some batter in mini-loaf pans so that your child has her very own bread. There is no need to sift the flour. As your child gets older, try using a wooden spoon to sift the whole wheat pastry flour by pressing it through a strainer. After the flour passes through the strainer, you will see the remaining small bits of whole grain. This is what makes it different from processed flour. Meanwhile, there is no need to sift! Just mix, bake, and enjoy!

3 ripe bananas

2 beaten eggs

¾ cup sugar

1 teaspoon vanilla

1 cup applesauce

2 cups whole wheat pastry flour
   or unbleached flour
Pinch of salt
1 teaspoon baking soda
Chocolate chips, optional

1. Preheat oven to 350° F.
2. Mash the bananas in a large mixing bowl.
3. Beat the eggs lightly and add to the bananas.
4. Add sugar, vanilla, and applesauce, and mix all ingredients.
5. Add flour, salt, and baking powder, and combine completely. Add chocolate chips if using.
6. Pour batter into greased loaf pans.
7. Bake 1 hour if making a larger 9-by-5 loaf or for ½ to ¾ hour if using smaller-size pans.

When you make salad, enlist your children to tear the lettuce and do the tossing! These are perfect for encouraging young children to have fun, be involved, and get their hands and arms moving. Keep a couple of large spoons or salad tossers for them to use.

If a recipe calls for cornflake or graham cracker crumbs, your child can make them easily. Place the ingredient in a small sealed plastic bag and use a rolling pin to crush it into crumbs.

Banana Oatmeal Cookies

These cookies are delicious and contain no dairy, eggs, or fats. They are sweetened mostly with bananas and applesauce. Mashing bananas and stirring in the rough oats fills your mixing bowl with great textures. Add in raisins, nuts, chocolate chips, or pieces of dried fruits to make banana oatmeal cookies just the way you like them!

2½ cups unbleached flour
   (or 1 cup whole wheat pastry flour and
   1½ cups unbleached flour)
2½ cups rolled oats (not instant)
1½ -2 teaspoons cinnamon
1 teaspoon baking soda
2 bananas
½ cup applesauce
1 teaspoon vanilla
½ -¾ cup sugar
Raisins, nuts, chocolate chips,
   dried fruits, optional

1. Preheat oven to 350° F.
2. In a large mixing bowl, stir together the flour, oats, cinnamon, and baking soda.
3. In another bowl, mash the bananas until smooth.
4. Add the applesauce, vanilla, and sugar to the mashed bananas and mix until smooth.
5. Pour the banana mixture into the dry ingredients and combine thoroughly.
6. Stir in any optional ingredients you choose.
7. Use a tablespoon to spoon out the dough for your cookies and place them on a greased cookie sheet. Press down each cookie lightly to shape it.
8. Bake 12 to 14 minutes.

Bread Sculpture

Take out your biggest mixing bowl and get ready for a great time. Bread sculpture keeps lots of small hands busy. Your children will measure, mix, and knead the dough and then use it to create imaginative shapes, letters, and creatures. They will see yeast in action as they watch their dough sculptures rise. Working dough offers young children real hands-on cooking experience. Consider making bread sculptures when friends come to visit.

1 package yeast

2 cups warm water

3 tablespoons honey

2 teaspoons salt

½ cup oil

7 cups unbleached flour

1. Preheat oven to 350° F.
2. In a very large bowl, mix yeast and warm water with honey. Let stand for five minutes.
3. Add salt, oil, and flour to the yeast mixture and combine until dough is formed. If the dough is sticky, add more flour a little bit at a time.
4. Knead the dough until it is smooth.
5. Tear off various sized pieces and create dough sculptures that can lie flat.
6. Place the sculptures on a cookie sheet lined with aluminum foil.
7. Let the sculptures rise 20 minutes.
8. Bake about 20 to 30 minutes, depending on the size of the sculptures. The bread should be golden when done.

Keep your eyes open for child-sized rolling pins to use for cooking or art. A good alternative is the one-inch cylinder from a set of wooden building blocks or a 6-to 8-inch long dowel from the hardware store.

Broccoli Cheese Casserole

Broccoli is a favorite vegetable for many children. This tasty casserole mixes it with cheese for a main course or side dish your family can enjoy. On a weekend morning, it is easy to make together and have it ready for lunch.

3 cups cooked chopped broccoli,
   either fresh or frozen
½ cup grated cheddar cheese
½ cup low-fat mayonnaise
½ cup low-fat cottage cheese
1 egg
5 to 6 saltine crackers
Paprika

1. Preheat oven to 375° F.
2. Combine broccoli, cheeses, mayonnaise, and egg in a bowl. Mix well.
3. Grease a loaf pan. Pour in broccoli mixture.
4. Place crackers in a re-sealable plastic bag and crumble them by squeezing or pounding the bag or using a rolling pin.
5. Pour the coarsely crumbled crackers on top of the broccoli mixture. Sprinkle with paprika.
6. Bake about 30 minutes until casserole is firm and lightly brown.

Cheese Pastries

Get your hands and rolling pins ready to work. This is a great recipe to make with more than one child and encourages your children to try different cheeses. Be sure to sample each cheese along the way. Enjoy these pastries when still warm and fresh from the oven.

1 cup unbleached flour
¼ cup butter at room temperature
½ cup (2 ounces) shredded cheese
   (Muenster, Cheddar, Swiss)
Cold water

1. Preheat oven to 350° F.
2. Sift the flour.
3. Add the butter and use a fork to combine.
4. Add cheese and 1 tablespoon cold water. Mix ingredients together. Hands work best for this mixing.
5. Continue to add water a little at a time until dough sticks together but is not soggy. Add more flour if the dough becomes sticky.
6. Roll out to ½-inch thickness, and cut into strips or roll coils with your hands.
7. Place on greased cookie sheet.
8. Bake 15 minutes or until brown and crispy.

Sometimes it is helpful to pre-measure ingredients so that they are ready to use and easier to handle. Paper cups work well as containers for pre-measured ingredients.

Chocolate Dipping

Here is a way to have a sweet taste of chocolate combined with other good foods. Chocolate dipping is fun and easy to do with more than one child. You can serve some chocolate-dipped fruits that your child has made for a wonderful dessert at a family holiday dinner. Remember to lick the chocolate drips along the way.

Semisweet chocolate (morsels or baking chocolate)

Vegetable oil

Foods to dip:

Strawberries with stems on, washed lightly and dried

Banana pieces

Orange sections

Dried apricots

Pretzels—sticks or twists

1. Line a cookie sheet or large platter with waxed paper.
2. Prepare foods for dipping.
3. Melt chocolate in microwave and stir in a few drops of vegetable oil if it is too thick. Let chocolate cool so it is not too hot to handle.
4. Dip foods one by one in the chocolate, shake off the excess, and lay each piece on the waxed paper to cool.
5. Once they are cooled and the chocolate has formed a coating, you can lift the pieces easily off of the waxed paper to eat or serve.

While cooking, young children love to experience the different tastes, textures, and aromas of the ingredients. Sampling along the way is part of the fun. Avoid tasting anything with raw egg in it.

Lasagna

Homemade lasagna will be the center of attention at your family dinner table as your children proudly spoon out portions on each plate. Assembling lasagna layers is great fun as they follow the "sauce, noodle, cheese" sequence. Your lasagna will be a personal creation and perhaps a bit different every time. "Ready to bake" lasagna noodles are easy to use and will require more sauce. You can vary the seasonings and use more or less of the cheeses depending on your family's taste.

Make your lasagna even more nutritious by adding vegetables. Frozen peas or defrosted chopped broccoli or spinach can be mixed into the ricotta mixture or sauce. Fresh vegetables such as eggplant, zucchini, mushrooms, tomatoes, red peppers, and onions can be lightly sautéed or steamed and added as well.

2 cups low fat ricotta cheese

½ cup grated Parmesan cheese

½ teaspoon salt

1½ teaspoons oregano

2 large jars prepared spaghetti sauce

Ready to bake lasagna noodles

   (or cooked lasagna noodles)

2 cups chopped

   or shredded low-fat mozzarella cheese

¼ cup grated Parmesan cheese

   to sprinkle on top

1. Preheat oven to 350° F.

2. Mix together ricotta, Parmesan, salt, and oregano.

3. Grease a deep 9-by-13 baking pan or a disposable aluminum lasagna pan with oil and pour a thin layer of sauce to cover the bottom.

4. Add a layer of noodles.

5. Next, add a layer of ricotta cheese mixture, more sauce, and then mozzarella cheese.

6. Repeat with more layers of noodles, sauce, and cheeses, ending with noodles about ½ inch from the top of the pan.

7. Cover top noodles with more sauce and sprinkle with Parmesan.

8. Bake 45 minutes uncovered and let stand 15 minutes before cutting.

Children love to find something they made themselves in their backpacks and lunchboxes. Include some of their "home cooking" to offer a larger variety of lunch and snack choices.

Noodle Pudding

This traditional dish has many variations, and you may come across other versions to try. There is a lot for your children to do however you make it, with broad or thin noodles, more or less sweet, with fruit or without, extra cinnamon or a splash of vanilla. Experiment to discover how your family enjoys it. This recipe will keep you busy cooking and enjoying the wonderful aroma while it bakes. Serve it as a main course, side dish, or dessert to have a big hit.

1 pound broad noodles, cooked

1 pound low-fat cottage cheese

2 cups low-fat sour cream

4 eggs

1 cup low-fat milk

½ cup butter cut in small pieces

¼ cup sugar

½ teaspoon salt

½ cup canned crushed pineapple, drained

1 cup crushed cornflakes

1 teaspoon cinnamon

¼ cup brown sugar

1. Preheat oven to 350° F.
2. Grease 9-by-13 baking dish.
3. Boil and drain the noodles. This job is for grownups.
4. Mix together the cottage cheese, sour cream, eggs, milk, butter, sugar, and salt.
5. Stir in the pineapple.
6. Add the noodles to the mixture, combine thoroughly, and pour into the baking dish.
7. Crush cornflakes and combine with cinnamon and brown sugar to make topping.
8. Sprinkle topping evenly over the noodles.
9. Bake 1 to 1¼ hours.

Pasta and Vegetable Salad

Here is a nutritious dish for lunch, dinner, picnics, and snacks. Vary it each time using different shaped and colored pastas, the vegetables you have on hand or what is currently in season, and your favorite dressings. Adding legumes such as beans and chickpeas makes it even more nutritious. Your children may suggest other vegetables to add to their pasta salad.

To soften vegetables such as carrots, broccoli, and green beans for easier cutting, put them in boiling water for a couple of minutes. If you use frozen peas or corn, add them to the boiling pasta for the last few minutes of cooking.

Dried pasta of various shapes

Assorted vegetables such as green beans, carrots, peppers, cherry tomatoes, mushrooms, broccoli, peas, corn

Legumes such as beans and chickpeas

Salad dressing

1. Cook and drain the pasta. This job is for grownups.
2. Put the pasta into a large mixing bowl.
3. Cut vegetables into bite-size pieces and add to drained pasta. Mix together.
4. Pour in salad dressing and toss thoroughly.
5. Serve at room temperature or chill and serve cold.

Pizza

Pizza is a popular food for many families and is fun to make. Children especially enjoy working with the dough and watching its elasticity as it stretches and contracts. Making pizza is a great activity with a group of children as each child chooses his favorite toppings. If you make pizza often, consider adding a pizza pan to your collection of kitchen equipment.

Ready-made pizza dough is available in the supermarket or at your local pizza restaurant. If you prefer to make it yourself, here is a recipe:

2 cups unbleached flour

2 tablespoons baking powder

1 teaspoon salt

⅔ cup milk

¼ cup vegetable oil

Mix the ingredients and knead until smooth. This recipe makes enough for two pizzas.

To make your pizza you need:

½ cup grated Parmesan cheese

½ pound shredded mozzarella cheese

Chopped vegetables including green or
    red peppers, mushrooms, broccoli,
    or spinach

Dough

Olive oil

1 cup tomato or pizza sauce

½ teaspoon oregano

1. Preheat oven to 425° F.
2. Grate the Parmesan and shred the mozzarella. Set aside.
3. Chop the vegetables. Set aside.
4. Stretch, pound, and knead the dough. Divide into two pieces. Use a rolling pin to flatten each piece. The pizza does not have to be perfectly round.
5. Place dough on greased pizza pan or cookie sheet.
6. Turn up the edge of the dough all the way around. Brush with a small amount of oil.
7. Spoon the tomato sauce onto the dough.
8. Shake oregano onto the sauce.
9. Spread the cheeses and vegetables on top.
10. Bake for 20 to 25 minutes.

Pretzels

Knead, pull, stretch, squeeze, and roll until it is time to pop your pretzels into the oven. Make tasty pretzel shapes or use the dough to create snakes, letters, or whatever you like. This recipe is terrific to do with more than one child and children of different ages. Everyone, grownups included, will love the feel of this dough.

2 packages dry yeast

1½ cups warm water

2 tablespoons sugar

1 teaspoon salt

1 cup whole wheat flour

3 cups unbleached flour

1 beaten egg

1. Preheat oven to 425° F.

2. In a large bowl, mix the yeast and water together and let stand for five minutes.

3. Add sugar and mix.

4. Add salt and both flours and mix well.

5. Sprinkle flour on the table or on a cutting board. Place the dough on the floured surface and knead for five minutes.

6. Break off pieces of dough and roll them into coils for twisting into pretzels.

7. Place on ungreased cookie sheet spaced 2 inches apart.

8. Brush the dough with the beaten egg and sprinkle with salt.

9. Bake 12 to 15 minutes, until golden brown.

Thanksgiving Stuffing

Include your children in the Thanksgiving preparations or make this recipe anytime as stuffing or a side dish. Be inventive by adding other vegetables or dried fruits according to your family's taste. You can double or triple the recipe as needed.

1 loaf day old Italian bread

4 small apples

4 large mushrooms

1 small bunch parsley

2 stalks celery

½ teaspoon poultry seasoning

2 eggs

1 stick melted margarine or butter

Raisins, green pepper, peas, optional

1. Preheat the oven to 350° F.

2. Tear bread into small pieces in a large bowl.

3. Chop apples, mushrooms, parsley, and celery.

4. Add to the bread and mix.

5. Mix in the seasoning and combine thoroughly.

6. Beat the eggs and add, along with the melted margarine, to the bread mixture and use to stuff your turkey. Add any optional ingredients.

7. For a side dish, grease an 8-by-8 pan, spoon the stuffing mixture into the pan and bake 30 minutes.

Thumbprint Cookies

Easy to make and delicious to eat, children love making their thumbprints in each and every cookie.

1 egg yolk

½ cup confectioner's sugar

½ pound butter, at room temperature

2 cups flour

Jelly

1. Preheat oven to 350° F.
2. Mix egg yolk, sugar, and butter in a large mixing bowl.
3. Add flour, mix completely, and form into a large ball.
4. One at a time, break off small, tablespoon-sized pieces.
5. Flatten each piece with the palm of the hand and place on a greased cookie sheet, leaving space between each one. Press a fork into each cookie to make a design in the dough.
6. Have your children make a thumbprint in the center of each cookie by pushing their thumbs into the dough.
7. Fill each thumbprint with a ½ teaspoon of jelly.
8. Bake about 20 minutes.
9. Cool thoroughly before eating because the jelly will be steaming hot.

Vegetable Cheese Bake

Hot and delicious, this one-dish meal is easy to make. You and your children can experiment with different cheeses and vegetables, and find some winning combinations. Add a green salad for a nutritious family meal.

1 cup low-fat cottage cheese

1 cup low-fat sour cream

2 tablespoons flour

2 eggs

½ teaspoon salt

¼ teaspoon black pepper

¾ cup shredded mozzarella, cheddar, or Parmesan

3 cups frozen mixed vegetables thawed

½ cup breadcrumbs

1. Preheat oven to 350° F.
2. In a large bowl, mix together cottage cheese, sour cream, flour, eggs, salt, and pepper.
3. Add ½ cup of the shredded cheese and vegetables and mix.
4. Pour into a greased baking pan.
5. Sprinkle remaining cheese and breadcrumbs on top.
6. Bake about 45 minutes until bubbly and golden brown. Let sit 15 minutes before serving.

When a child-sized cooking utensil is not available, improvise. Wooden tongue depressors make great spreaders, and plastic serrated knives can be used for cutting.

> If your cake does not rise or comes out crooked, that is just fine! It is making it together that matters the most.

Vegetable Frittata

It is time to take out your pie plate and use it in a new way. Here is a pie to eat as a main course rather than as a dessert!

2 tablespoons oil

2 cups partially cooked broccoli

1 scallion

1 zucchini

1 red pepper

½ cup sliced mushrooms

¼ cup grated sharp cheddar cheese

6 slightly beaten eggs

1. Preheat oven to 400° F.
2. Grease an 8 or 9-inch pie plate with the oil.
3. Cut the vegetables and put them into the greased pie plate.
4. Mix cheese and eggs and season with salt and pepper.
5. Pour cheese and egg mixture over vegetables.
6. Bake for 20 to 30 minutes until eggs have puffed and center of the frittata is set.

Zucchini Bread

Your children may be surprised to see a vegetable used this way. A slice of zucchini bread with some yogurt and fruit is a terrific snack, breakfast, or lunchbox addition.

3 cups sifted unbleached flour

1½ teaspoons cinnamon

1 teaspoon baking soda

1 teaspoon salt

¼ teaspoon baking powder

2 cups sugar

1 cup oil

3 beaten eggs

1 tablespoon vanilla

2 cups grated zucchini

1. Preheat oven to 350° F.
2. In a large bowl, combine dry ingredients.
3. Add remaining ingredients and mix well.
4. Place in two greased 9-by-5-by-3 inch loaf pans
5. Bake 1 hour.

While You Are In the Kitchen

MAKE YOUR OWN COOKIE TIN

Your children are at the beginning of their cookie-baking years, and many dozens of cookies will be coming out of your oven. Having their own special cookie tins to store their cookies adds to the fun. Discount and houseware stores sell undecorated solid-color tins in various sizes. Gather some permanent colored markers and favorite stickers and set your baker to work. Another way to decorate is to cut a piece of paper the shape of the lid, design it, and attach it to the top of the tin with clear contact paper. Young children also enjoy having their names on their tins. Writing the date on the bottom of the tin will give you all great pleasure when you look back at this unique "family heirloom" in the future. Tins decorated by your children and filled with their home-baked cookies make special gifts. This is also a great birthday party activity, and each guest will leave with a special tin.

TIME FOR A PICNIC!

It is time for your children to plan the picnic and make the food—with your help, of course. Choose a picnic destination as close as your own backyard or local park. Indoor picnics with a plastic tablecloth on the living room floor are also great fun, especially on rainy or wintry days. Talk together about what your children would like to prepare so that everyone has something good to eat and not only dessert! It can be as basic as sandwiches and homemade cookies or might include a few more of their favorite recipes. Help them to make it, pack it, and enjoy the picnic they have planned and prepared.

Cook together! When you are preparing meals, look for jobs your children can do to help. They can clean the green beans, shell the peas, shred the cheese, and husk the corn!

START YOUR OWN COOKBOOK

Your young chefs will be trying many recipes as they spend more time cooking and learning about food. Making their own personal cookbook gives them a way to save the recipes they enjoy. Start with a loose-leaf binder and plastic page holders. These work well for young children to slip in the recipes they collect. Your children can create a "title page" for their cookbooks and decorate recipe pages if they choose. As their cookbooks grow, they can reorganize the recipes in new ways.

You may want to create a computerized version of your child's cookbook. Print out the pages so that your children can add them to their cookbook binders. An "actual" cookbook is really their own. They can always add new recipes, browse through the pages, open it on the kitchen counter when they get ready to cook, and see it get bigger over time.

> As your children get ready to read, add clearly written labels to your food containers. They will begin to recognize "flour," "sugar," "raisins," "cinnamon," and many other words that you enjoy using together.

APRONS AND PLACEMATS

Be on the lookout for white or light solid-colored cloth aprons and placemats that your children can decorate with fabric crayons or permanent markers. They can make one of their very own or a set for the entire family and add to their fun in the kitchen.

COOKIE AND LEMONADE STANDS

After your children turn five, they might be ready for their first "Cookie and Lemonade Stand." Older children are more able to do the planning and preparation. This traditional favorite is great fun and a valuable opportunity to learn about money and math. It will need ongoing grownup involvement. The idea will likely come from your children, who learn about it from their friends or see a stand in the neighborhood. They may want to earn money to buy something special for themselves or make a contribution to an important cause.

Help your children plan their stand. Together, bake a big batch of cookies, prepare plenty of lemonade, and gather napkins and cups. Your children can make a big sign listing what they are selling and what it costs. Sign making is a great early reading activity. Keep the pricing simple. Be sure to have a container with a lid for the money. Review the names and value of pennies, nickels, dimes, quarters, and dollars. Stay with your children to help collect money and give the right change. Think carefully about a location for the stand. Outside your home might be the perfect spot. If not, look for a place that has some steady foot traffic but is not overwhelmingly busy.

MAKE YOUR OWN SNACK LIST

Healthy, delicious snacks are easy to find to move beyond cookies, chips, and other highly processed foods. Making snacks together is fun and a chance to chat about healthy nutrition. These are important years to get off to a good start.

Keeping your own list of family favorite snacks is a great way to begin. Together, make a list of healthy snack foods. You can write the words and glue on labels from the foods that so your child can "read" the list. Include everything on your list, even cookies and chips, offering balance and variety. Keep your snack list handy in the kitchen so that your children can see it. Help your children be open to new possibilities and more adventurous eating. Your list will get longer as all of you learn about and taste new foods at school, restaurants, and the homes of friends. Use your imagination and be creative as your list grows.

Here are some ideas to begin:

- Fruit
- Crackers
- Cheese
- Cookies
- Granola
- Hard-boiled eggs
- Raw vegetables and dips
- Peanut butter (or other nut butters) with apple, crackers, vegetables, or whole grain bread
- Applesauce
- Cereal—dry or with milk or fruit
- English muffin pizzas
- Yogurt
- Fresh fruit kabobs
- Whole wheat breadsticks
- Dried fruit
- Pretzels
- Sandwiches
- Fruit ice pops
- Soup

Looking Ahead

~~~~~~~~~~

Enjoy **WONDERPLAY, TOO!** Find the moments that work best for you. It may be a weekend afternoon set aside and planned for family time. Or it could be when everyday chores and demands of children, home, and work are busiest, and you spontaneously shift gears to re-energize and have fun together. Whether you use *Wonderplay, Too!* all the time or every so often, you are creating memorable experiences to enjoy with your family.

Looking ahead as your children grow, their individual interests and preferences will become more defined. Follow their lead as they suggest what they would like to do. Revisit old favorites and explore new possibilities. There are more hats to make, beans to sprout, rocks to collect, and murals to paint. Keep *Wonderplay, Too!* handy as it will continue to offer you and your children ideas and activities for more great times together.

Acknowledgments

Wonderplay, Too! is infused with the expertise, vision, and creativity of the 92nd Street Y's remarkable staff whose collaborative efforts make the Y a wonderful place for young children and their families. We would like to thank our colleagues for their generous support: Sally Tannen, Nancy Schulman, Ellen Birnbaum, Gaby Greenberg, Kelli Crosby, Juli Greenberg, Danny Pollack, Helen Conover, Dave Schmeltzer, Bob Gilson, Hanna Arie-Gaifman, Misty Pereira, Edward Henkel, Rachel Selekman, Menon Dwarka, Mirabai Holland, Teddy Fernandez, Susan Rosenbaum, Dena Warren, Roberta Willenken, Lynne Rosen, Susan Alexander, Jennifer Zebooker, Ilsa Lowe, Barry Goldberg, Allan Uribe, Amy Wahl, Steve Herman, and Rebecca Blake.

At the 92nd Street Y, we thank Sol Adler and Helaine Geismar Katz for their commitment to bringing *Wonderplay, Too!* to parents and children beyond the Y's doors. We are grateful for the efforts of Eleanor Goldhar, Alix Friedman, Shelly Felder, Howard Levine, and Sean Flannagan for their creative work on our behalf. Our friend and colleague, Karen Kolodny, has been helpful in many ways and we thank her for sharing her expertise. We want to acknowledge the continuing and cheerful encouragement from our many Y friends, especially Michael Kramberg, Marty Maskowitz, Joan Zoref, and Guy Giarrizzo. We also greatly appreciate the entire Goldman Center staff for their continuing enthusiasm and interest in this project as well as the May Center for keeping us healthy, fit, and energized.

We consider ourselves fortunate to have had the help of Juana Lee during the writing of *Wonderplay, Too!*. Her reliable, cheerful, and expert assistance are most appreciated.

We thank Maxine Berger, Jennifer Kasius, and Mark Smith for their efforts in bringing *Wonderplay, Too!* to print.

Thanks to our many friends and family for their good-natured understanding and interest. Special thanks to Max Cox.

And most important, we could not have brought *Wonderplay, Too!* from idea to printed page without Anna, Rek, Jay, Nico, Tim, Ali, and Luis. They supported us in many loving, uniquely personal, and much appreciated ways throughout the writing of this book. Once again, we thank them for always being in our corner.

—Fretta Reitzes and Beth Teitelman